The People's History

Lynemouth

by

Neil Taylor

Lynemouth FC 1944-45. This fine team was probably the most successful side to play at Lynemouth. In one season they won four trophies, the Booth Cup, Ashington Hospital Cup, Blyth Knight Memorial Trophy and the Northumberland Senior Cup. Many of them had Football League experience. Back: J. Hindmarsh, W. Brown, Danny Staines, R. Messenger, Bill Peary, Jim Tomlin, Matty Richardson, Bob Youngs and Joe Hogg. Front: George (Dusty) Down, Bob Farrington, Bill Tait, R. Withington, Dicky Freeman.

Front cover: Lynemouth Rose Queen, *circa* 1932. The Rose Queen that year was Nellie Hogg. Her award was presented by Mrs Skene. Other girls in the competition that year included: Elsie Medlen, Nancy McLean, Annie McQuillan, Isobel Hogg, Betty Spowart, Jean Hogg, Veronica O'Kane and Annie Teasdale.

Copyright © Neil Taylor 1999

First published in 1999 by

The People's History Ltd
Suite 1
Byron House
Seaham Grange Business Park
Seaham
Co. Durham
SR7 0PY

ISBN 1 902527 42 9

Contents

The Pit Village

As a child when I lay warm in bed,
I listened to the sound of the midnight tread
Of heavy boots on the cobbled street.
The hushed voices of men passing by on their
way to a hidden world
As the village rests.

Moonlight shadows around my window,
The evening sky filled with winking stars,
Rooftops sparkled row on row thick keen with
frost,
A hunting owl called from far off wood
clear and lingering on the still night air,
As the village sleeps.

Pithead buzzers tell the time
Signal bells shatter the dreaming world,
Steam trains whistle and hiss impatiently
in crowded sidings,
work is imminent,
As the village dreams.

In the morning time children play
in the powdered snow,
Mothers bustle and chatter,
then hurry on their way
to meet with friends in the busy streets,
As the village wakes.

And in the early evening,
when the sun slips below velvet hills,
The first lights glow in warm houses,
Where kinfolk gather to share the feasted table
and proud fathers in time honoured fashion
say grace to restless wide eyed children.
As the village smiles.

Today the cobbled ways lie bare,
No men pass by in the night,
The trains were silent long ago,
and the pithead weathers in the winter winds.
A hunting owl still calls
But no one hears,
As the village weeps.

Neil Taylor

Introduction

While it is true that the recording of dates and events is essential in the Social History of any area, this account gives a more personal insight into the Lynemouth mining community from the early part of the twentieth century.

The idea of a book to document the events of early Lynemouth came after the death of my mother in 1996. There were so few of her friends still living, and even less of the original village residents, that I wondered if perhaps some day the early years would be forgotten.

When an old friend of mine returned to live in the village in 1997 he brought with him many of his father's photographs and memories. This was the deciding factor, 'the die was cast', now work on a book would begin.

I felt it necessary to involve as many of the villagers as possible to contribute text or photographs so that the end product really would be a 'People's History'. My own memories are happy ones, from the Second World War as a child and schooldays and on to life boys, scouts and chapel. Then to my working years at Ellington Colliery and Alcan when football, leeks and pigeons became a part of my life.

The special bond that existed in mining communities was forged from the early years of private coal owners, low wages and spartan living and working conditions where every family had precious little to exist and to help their neighbour in distress became a natural instinct. Only Ellington Colliery remains as a working reminder of Ashington Coal Company's five pits in the area.

I have spent countless hours talking, interviewing and sharing the good company of many people connected with Lynemouth, hearing humorous and sad stories. It has been a rewarding experience. The most authentic sources available have been used to compile this work.

It was purely coincidental that this book be published for the 'Millennium'. As this has happened take a look back with me at a pit village of the twentieth century at 'Lynemouth From The Inside'.

Early History

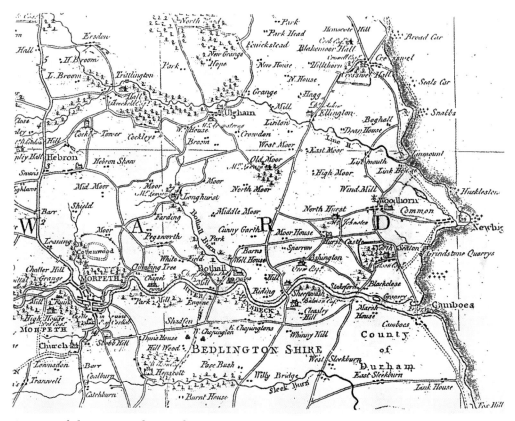

A map of the county by Andrew Armstrong 1769.

The small hamlet of Linmouth is how Haselhurst describes the village in his history of Northumberland. Swampy land with springs rising from the earth. This is the reason that the low lying area was of little use for agriculture.

The hamlet consisted of four houses – Linmouth Farm, Park House, Linmouth Cottage and Dene House, which was later part of the Cresswell Estate.

The spelling of the name Lynemouth as we know it today was not formulated until the first part of the twentieth century. The early records show it as Linmouth, Linemouth or Linmuwe in the Parish of Wodehorn.

However, there is no doubt that the name is derived from the river Lyne which rises on Longhorsley Moor to the west and flows serenely to its meeting with the North Sea at Lynemouth Bay.

A study of the land to the south of the river, suggests that the Lyne once flowed there in prehistoric times and entered the sea at Newbiggin Bay.

The earliest references to Linmuwe are in 1240 when John De Baliol held parcels of land in Newbiggang, Wodehorn and Linmuwe with Hurst. The same John De Baliol was then the Regent of Scotland and founder of the famous Baliol College Oxford. This land was given in return for military service.

A more recent discovery is that from the time of Richard II to that of Queen Elizabeth, land was forfeited from the Barony of Balliol in 1388 to the

Nevilles o Raby who then owned much of the area around Linmuwe. This is typical of those times in the Middle Ages when grants of land would be accorded to the feudal Barons who happened to be in the Crown's favour at that time. The next recorded evidence is that Ralph de ure owned land in the area, and he died in the reign of Henry V.

In 1628, Mercers Company of London made purchases of tithed land in Linmouth. William Horsley was a land owner in 1663 and assessed for rates. Then in 1721 a Dr Watson owned an estate which he left to his daughter on his death.

The main land owner in the early part of the nineteenth century was Mr Atkinson a JP from Newcastle whose estate amounted to 315 acres. There is also a reference to Mr Bradford who married Mr Atkinson's niece and he owned parcels of land in the parish in 1832.

In 1900, Ashington Coal Company purchased large tracts of land in the area. Reserves of coal had been discovered in their borings, and therefore a new Lynemouth evolved, centred around the Coal Industry. It was 1909 when the first shaft was sunk at Ellington Colliery and rows of colliery houses appeared there to house miners and their families. Ashington Coal Company then commenced to build a mining village at Lynemouth and the first houses were occupied in October 1923. It was their intention to open up Lynemouth Colliery, but then came the general strike of 1926, this and other reasons resulted in Lynemouth not producing coal until 1934. This meant that the first miners in Lynemouth village worked at Ellington Colliery.

In 1921 there was only twenty-two people in four houses recorded living in the village, by 1926 there was 520 houses and a population of 2,000. In 1925 a cemetery and the Anglican Church were dedicated. Shops appeared to serve the growing community from 1924, and the Welfare sports ground opened the same year. The Miners' Institute opened and Lynemouth Hotel commenced trading in 1925. Ashington Co-operative society had premises open for business in 1925. The County Primary School was officially declared open on the 3rd May 1926 which was the first day of the General Strike. The Primitive Methodist Hall opened for worship in 1927. Lynemouth was by now growing apace and continued to do so until the 1950s.

Lynemouth in 1924.

Acknowledgements

A book of this nature would not have been possible without the help of many people who have supplied me with photographs and information of family, places and events in and around Lynemouth.

To Alan Youngs for his excellent work on the two collieries, a theme deserving a book of its own. To my son Neil who converted my long hand text to computer and disc, his assistance was crucial in producing this work. Lynemouth School who gave me ready access to their records. Lynemouth Parish Council for their files. Lynemouth Institute for their meetings records. Tom Quenet, Methodist Minister, for access to Willie Barron's notes. Lynemouth Church Council and members for information. To Jim Hindmarsh for the cemetery history. To Maurice Conn for his early Ellington records and Tom Cowan for Ashington Coal Company books. To Joe Hogg for his detailed information on Lynemouth and Ellington Band. To Mike Kirkup for inspiration and information.

The late George Sweet for ACC volumes, Mr & Mrs Jack Wyness, Brian George, Jim Hume, George Taylor, Harry & Mary Bryan, Alan Fairfax, Tom Lister, Tommy O'Keefe, Eddie Liddell, Archie Herron, Gillian Thompson, Jim Gargett, Alan Reed, David Crawford, Albert Reed, George Stewart, George Brown, Ernie Baker, Peggy Nicholson, Emily Harding, Mrs Prior, Bill Johnstone, Jack & Jim Simpson, Alan Simpson, Sid Waddell, Ritchie Stafford, Jacky Herron, Eleanor Tuck, Bill & Iris Foster, Charlie & Ruth Dawson, Frank Wyness, Paul Scott, Ron Fleming, Irene Tindale, Jane Miles, Tom Henderson, Tom Dent, Albert Wilkie, Jack Graham, Irene Smail, Joan Brodie, Olive Brown, Joyce Getty, Yvonne Casson, Cynthia Rough, Stan Elliot, Joyce Beattie, Ken & Jack Spratt, Chris Foster, John Talbot, Mary Preston, Matty Brough, Malcolm Musgrove, Sylvia Mitchinson, Jos Hanson, Mrs Sewell, Jack Cochrane, Bob Huntley, George Dunn, Ron & Val Brotherton, Bob Mavin, Matty Willis, Eleanor Paynter, Nancy Wilkinson, Andrea Taylor, Jean Morris and my wife Mary. To anyone who I may have missed My sincere apologies, but a personal thanks will be given to all.

Scouts have an answer to many problems and did on this occasion, building a bridge across a burn to carry supplies, *circa* 1960. Testing the bridge are, left to right: Tom Rankin, Tom Horn, Brian Hume, Andrew Hyslop and Michael Bell.

VILLAGE AT WORK

Travelling outbye by endless rope haulage, undermanagers Bill Allison and Lal Bell on a flat tram, while the ordinary pit lads sit in tubs, Ellington Colliery, *circa* 1930s.

Rail Link

John Talbot of Oxford has a passionate interest in North East Colliery railways and signalling systems. Here is John's account of the early Ellington and Lynemouth rail link:

The branch railway from the Linton to Ellington colliery was set out in July 1907, and the railhead reached the site of the pit on 10th October 1908. The branch was single track, and the signalling to deal with the coal companies' passenger and coal trains, and North Eastern Railways coal traffic, was introduced by 25th June 1912.

The passenger platform at Ellington was in the vicinity of the workshop yard. By 1921 a replacement passenger line and platform had been built nearer the public road. In December 1925 a new signal box was planned further away from the colliery where another branch to Lynemouth would diverge, this would be double track and the existing branch would be enhanced from single to double track. This box was in full operation by 30th June 1926, although it is not known how much use was made of the Lynemouth route initially.

Between Ellington and Lynemouth collieries the Ashington Coal Company provided two road overbridges, the only ones ever to be built on the system. These avoided manned gates, warning systems or coupling trains.

On 24th February 1936 the double line from Ellington to Lynemouth was altered to become two single lines, one for the colliery company and the other for the main line engines and trains.

The NER sent Bill Roberts, a foreman signal fitter, from York to Ashington to supervise the early signalling on the line, and he stayed on in Ashington still working with the NCB railway signals until 1952.

Mr J.D. Morton was Ashington Coal Company's Area Electrical Engineer, who later became head of European Mining for Siemans-Schuckert. Mr Morton's talents and Bill Roberts' experience made a good combination to proceed with a pioneering signalling system for the technically advanced colliery.

Sinkers and loco pictured at Ellington in 1909.

The Two Pits

by Alan F. Youngs

The story of Lynemouth as a mining village is essentially the story of the two collieries that sustained it. The development of the village from 1923 is the story of Ashington Coal Company and also the people of the village both old and young into whose hands the future of the model village was given.

Ellington Colliery (1909-1947)

In June 1909 work commenced on the sinking of Ellington Colliery last but one of ACC's five mines in the area. Ellington and later Lynemouth would be the only two to exploit the seaward reserves of coal within the company's thirty-seven square mile royalty, situated two and a half miles north east of Ashington and half a mile south of Ellington village. Borehole samples had shown the existence of six major coal seams.

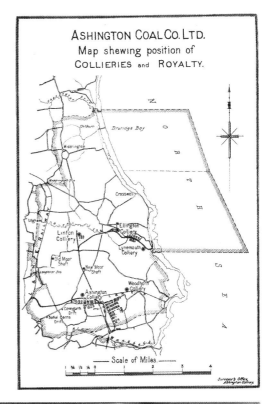

Below: The first sod was cut at No 1 shaft by Mr Francis Priestman, ACC director, on the 14th June 1909, quickly followed by No 2 and 3 shafts. In October 1910 the first coals were drawn from the yard seam.

Ellington Colliery in 1912 showing No 1 shaft heapstead and full coal wagons. The most modern mining equipment was introduced and Ellington developed rapidly over the next twenty years, justifying the decision of the company to sink the mine in this area. One factor was evident, the lack of any sizeable community to house the work force. Miners travelled from Ashington, Red Row, Chevington and Broomhill and many other areas.

The first shift down No 2 shaft, *circa* 1912. The man on the left is manager, Mr Weddell, centre back with hands on lapels is Tom Simpson.

The Ashington Coal Company built three rows of houses at Ellington Colliery in 1910 and commenced building a new model village at Lynemouth in 1921 where the first houses were occupied in 1923. The pit was developing rapidly and proving a success. On the surface the first pithead baths in the county opened in 1924. The three colliery rows can clearly be seen at the top.

Lynemouth in 1924. The houses on the north side are occupied and building well under way to the south. The pit manager's house is centre left and in the forefront is the Welfare Pavilion and grounds.

Ellington Colliery Pit Baths.

A typical soup kitchen at Ellington in 1921 during the 13 week strike.

Anything that burns will be picked from the heaps by these miners during the 1926 strike. The seven month strike in 1926 was a sad time for miners and their families with little state assistance. Soup kitchens were introduced and foraging for wood and coal a daily occurrence. The outcome of the strike saw men returning to work in November with a 10% cut in wages and a longer working week. Ellington prospered well after this and in 1927 the sinking of Lynemouth Colliery commenced one mile to the south of Ellington. Much of the labour force used in the sinking operation were miners from Woodhorn Colliery who worked with the regular sinking team.

Sinkers at work in Lynemouth No 2 shaft, 1927. On the right is Lynemouth man, Matty Davison.

Cookson's Folly

When the railway line was laid from Ellington colliery to Lynemouth in 1925-26, a decision on its route was taken which would affect Lynemouth forever. The intended course was to the south of the village, by the old road, across Lyne Burn and on past the Ellington Colliery manager's house at Parkroad.

However, Ashington Coal Company then altered the route, and drove the railway in a direct line through the centre of the village, which by then had 500 houses. The Ashington Coal Company man in charge of this operation was named Cookson, hence the name Cookson's Folly.

By day and night, Lynemouth was subjected to the noise and dirt of colliery cargo. 'Huffing', 'Puffing', 'Whistling' and 'Shunting', on the mile long railway.

The north side of the village supplied shops, churches and a school. The early settlers lived here and worked at Ellington Colliery. The south side provided recreation facilities and housed mainly Lynemouth Colliery families, whichever way one turned the problem was there – railway lines to cross, if not by the east or west road bridges, then by a more dangerous route. A direct attempt occasionally resulting in fatal consequences. The folly of the railway course resulted in delaying the village's real identity. The lines have gone now, but will always be there, in the memories of its older generations.

Looking east from the West Bridge, the wind is coming from the north and the people on the south side of the village will receive the full blast of the steam train smoke, *circa* 1950s.

Lynemouth Colliery (1927-1947)

Sinking operations of the two shafts started in July 1927. It would be 1934 before the first coals were drawn and the reasons for the delay are not clearly expressed by ACC. The early 1930s saw a steadily influx of miners from near and far, many were recruited from local collieries, almost all of the Brotherton family from Ashington came to work at the colliery and reside in the village. The Grahams from Haltwhistle arrived and their off-springs are evident today.

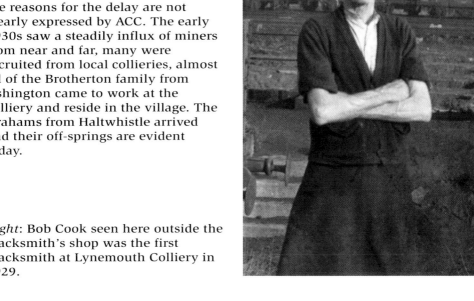

Right: Bob Cook seen here outside the blacksmith's shop was the first blacksmith at Lynemouth Colliery in 1929.

George Mavin picking and Denis Fail on composite work in Ellington's North West Diamond District. The initial ACC targets of 2,000 tons per day was not being met by 1947 from a work force of 730. The new Labour Government decided that the industry should be under state control and it was obvious a major reconstruction programme was needed. Expansive coal reserves of 123 million tons had been confirmed in undersea borings, the projected output would be 6,000 tons per day and equate to one and a half million tons a year ensuring the collieries future for over 65 years. New legislation on health and safety saw the introduction of a regulation that addressed the appalling safety record in the mining industry. Men had been losing their lives at a national average of three per day and substantially more being seriously injured. A five day week was introduced, shorter working hours and a week's holiday with improved wages. Thus began the most successful period the two pits would ever experience.

Lynemouth and Ellington Collieries produced outstanding first aid teams with a healthy rivalry existing between the two pits. *Above*: The successful Lynemouth Colliery St John Ambulance members 1958, included in back row are: Tommy Orr, George Mead and Bob Farrier. Centre row: Jim Graham, John Freeman, Albert Rogers, Ron Staines, Alan Youngs and Jim Jeffries. Front row: Bill Clancey, Alex Cummings, Horace Madeley. *Below*: The Ellington Colliery first aid team being presented with awards after winning the Northern (N&C) Senior First Aid final in 1955. Left to right: Chairman N&C Division, Bob Wright, Ernie Baker, Tom Thornton, Les Scott and Bill Barrass.

Reconstruction At Both Mines (1947-1956)

Lynemouth Colliery

The reconstruction at Lynemouth involved the pithead plant and new surface installations. Remodelling underground was centred around the coal transport system, this period saw the introduction of the first Joy Continuous Mining machines. By the late 1950s Lynemouth moved into a period of steady growth in output – its major reconstruction now complete.

A Joy Continuous Miner in operation at Lynemouth in the 1950s. Production units, as at Ellington, were mainly conventional long-wall faces, however in the 1940s new methods of extraction were discovered and the new cutting techniques such as the Arc-Shearer, which would pave the way to further development and bring the 'Gathering Arm Loader Shuttle Cars' and eventually the highly productive 'Continuous Miner'.

Ellington Colliery

Major reconstruction and remodelling work at Ellington began in 1949, although not on the scale as at Lynemouth, it cost over £1 million and involved upgrading of both surface and underground installations. The transport system received highest priority and it was hoped to increase production to 4,000 tons per day – one million tons per year and an expected pit life of 40 years. All untreated coal would be sent to a new central washery, transported by rail through the village of Lynemouth. New pithead baths, canteen medical centre and lamp cabin were built at this time. By mid 1954 the work was finished and output levels increased by 65% and by 1957 production had risen to 750,000 tons per year.

After Reconstruction At Both Collieries

For Lynemouth the years between 1960 and 1966 would be ones of record output with Ellington also increasing production with less units. At this time the most modern hi-tech machines available were introduced to the two pits, who were producing well in excess of two million tons a year. Expectations at that time were high until fate rudely intervened at Lynemouth Colliery in November 1966.

Lynemouth Pit On Fire (1964-1966)

In 1964 routine air samples at the mine suggested that all was not well as an increase in certain gases were detected. Minor heating was suspected in an area where main and diamond seams merged. As conditions worsened measures were taken to effect an air-tight seal. This failed and yet production continued at record levels. In 1966 conditions were so bad the fight was lost and on the 15th November the pit summarily closed which meant 1,800 men out of work. These men were employed at Longhirst, Woodhorn and Ellington Colliery. Plans were made to flood the mine the very next day to a level above the seat of the fire, but almost 100 ponies were still underground. A decision was made to reverse the ventilation fan on the surface for an hour or so to allow a rescue attempt. This was a brave decision considering the dangers involved in a pit which was on fire, but it worked and the ponies were saved, and the mine flooded with 200 million gallons of water from the sea and Lyne burn, Ashington, Woodhorn, Newbiggin and Ellington pits were also affected by the noxious gases from the fire as they had airways which were connected to Lynemouth Colliery. However conditions at these collieries stabilised in a short period of time.

Underground stables at Ellington during a visit from Coal Company officials and trainees, *circa* 1937.

Re-opening of Lynemouth Colliery

On the 14th December 1966 proposals were made to re-open the colliery by the area board. In March 1967 limited production commenced on the south side of the mine. Access to the productive north side meant the sinking of two ventilation shafts and the construction of a 1400 yards drift.

The new Bewick drift rises above the coast road to enter the Lynemouth complex, at the rear are the chimneys of the Alcan smelter. On 20th December 1967 the new drift was officially opened by Cecil Bewick, Area General Manager of NCB Area, hence the name Bewick drift. Ellington Colliery connected underground and coals transported to the washery at Lynemouth in 1968. By 1972 the two mines were again producing over two million tons a year with 3,000 men employed. In 1972 markets for the two pits increased greatly with the onset of the new Alcan Aluminium plant near to the Lynemouth Colliery, as the untreated small coal was ideal for the company's generating plant.

The Miners Strikes of the 1970s and '80s

A period of unrest in the industry during the 1970s fuelled the strikes of 1972 and 1974, called by the National Union of Mineworkers. A breakaway union was formed after a split in the NUM ranks which resolved in the formation of the UDM. It could be said that this sowed the seeds in the minds of the government at the time which would eventually result in the demise of the coal mining industry. The bitter year long strike of 1984/85 will forever be remembered in the village. As time progressed splits in the ranks appeared, workmen against workmen with family rivalries and loss of life-time friendships. A cruel and unpleasant time for all but the miners marched back to their pits with banners flying. As in 1926 nothing was gained but this time the Government decimated the coal industry by closing half the mines throughout the country. Legislation was put in place to limit the actions of trade unions and what future lay ahead was uncertain for any of the industry's mines.

A Northumberland Miners' Rally at Newcastle in 1984. The boy on his dad's shoulders plea for a future went unheard, the miners' grim faces tell the story. (Courtesy of George Swift Photography)

Ellington Combine

In 1983 Ellington & Lynemouth Collieries combined as one pit. This effectively meant the closure of Lynemouth. Ellington enjoyed super pit status and was named 'The Big E'. New sophisticated machines were introduced and in 1987 two million tons a year produced – an all-time record.

In the 1990s, natural gas and oil were taking over the generating markets. Electric output was no longer under state control. British Coal was extracting high standards from the remaining collieries, but there was no doubt that coal was in decline. After protracted negotiations British Coal decided to close the colliery in February 1994, and maintain on a care and maintenance basis.

Coal Privatisation

The pit came into the private sector when RJB Mining purchased the Big E in late 1994. Of the 2,000 plus employees before the take over, only 390 men are currently employed at the combine. Now at the once proud village, that had over 2,500 working at its two mines, those fortunate enough to gain re-employment are numbered in low double figures. At the time of writing, due to geological problems, RJB are looking to sell the colliery. Alas a mining village no more.

Once Coal Was King – Sadly No More.

Farming

In addition to the collieries in the Ashington Coal Company royalties in 1912 the company occupied 1,200 acres of farm land and owned a fine herd of dairy cows, which supplied a large proportion of the population with milk. By 1925 the acreage increased to 4,000 of which 1,500 acres were owned by the coal company. The rest was leased from the Crown, the Duke of Portland and other land owners. The increase in acreage came mainly after the sale of Cresswell Estate in 1924. Stock on the farms at that time included 1,200 head of cattle, 3,500 sheep and a total of 150 dairy cows. Additional land and stock meant more jobs for local people and many have been employed on the local farms at some time, be it full-time or helping out at corn harvest or potato picking. Most of the children from Boghall and the Grange attended Lynemouth School and this meant a two mile walk for the Dickinson, Mack, Brewis and the Hindmarsh families often in severe weather.

Right: Woodhorn Grange Farm manager's house. The Woodhorn Grange Farm buildings and cottages were demolished when Alcan leased the land, but the fine main house still stands and is used as a conference centre by British Alcan. Boghall cottages still remain and are tenanted, but the farm buildings are in a state of disrepair, vandals and thieves removing slate and stone at will.

Dene House Farm from the West Bridge. The farm was built around 1750 and is shown on a county map in 1769. Tenants in the 1800s were the Stamp family then the Proctor family are shown to have been residents in the early part of this century. After 1924 it became the agricultural repair centre for Ashington Coal Company Farms. The first blacksmith was a Mr Ellwood until Hugh Crawford in 1939. A master craftsman, Hugh repaired farm machinery, milking machines and made shoes for all the company's horses until 1960.

David Crawford remembers Dene House Farm: 'In the photograph (previous page), behind the water tower, are a line of wagons from which two hoppers of coal were fed, one of 'coal doubles' – for officials of the pit – and the other of 'singles' for the remaining householders entitled to the allowance. From this depot and weighbridge Lisle Downie delivered the coal with a Clydesdale drawn two wheeled farm cart, which was hinged and allowed the load to be tipped or shovelled directly into the coalhouse depending upon the status of the recipient.

To the left of the water tower a loading chute can be seen. Rail wagons full of moss litter from the bedding of the underground pit ponies were emptied here. This formed a huge heap of smelly manure which local boys used as a landing place when using the chute as a banana slide!

A local character who lived at Dene House was called Walter Brown or 'Watty' as he was better known. He lived with his wife Meggie in the original house – the one with the window bricked up to reduce the window tax imposed in bygone years. Watty worked on the farms on a roving commission, he drove a very powerful but slow Case tractor imported from America on 'Lease Lend' during the Second World War. The majority of his time was taken up going from farm to farm with a large threshing machine that was belt driven from his tractor. Watty would sit on his tractor going about 5 mph with a broken shanked clay pipe that had a steel cover to prevent sparks and ash flying into his eyes. He also had the bottom of his trousers tied with binder twine in an effort to stop mice from the haystacks running up his trouser legs, this was not always successful and it was not unusual for an escapee to be running around the kitchen vigorously pursued by his wife.'

The derelict farm and tower at Boghall.

Lynemouth Farm

Haselhurst in his History of the County describes Linmouth Farm. Armstrong's county map of 1769 shows buildings in this area. It seems a reasonable conclusion that the farm was built around the same time as the Dene House Farm about 1750. Certainly a working farm with foundations of the old buildings remained, these were demolished in the 1950s. Originally the two cottages, which are still tenanted, were single storey until 1930 then a second storey added using stone from Cresswell Hall. Originally tenants were the Halls then Reeds and now the Kent family. An interesting feature typical of many north country farm houses is the lack of windows to the north side, mainly for insulation purposes. This would have been beneficial in the early years when a 'window tax' was levied on the number of windows in the farm house.

Threshing at Boghall in
1950, Tommy Pringle is
centre bottom.

Stan Elliot and Norma on
the corn cart at Boghall in
1957.

Snow clearing at the grange in 1947. Left to right: Bob Mack, Ken Spratt, Bob Bell, Doreen Mack, unknown and Tom Hudson. The winter did no harm to the sheep which had to be dug out daily as they won prizes at the local mart in 1947.

Jim and Chris Proctor with daughter Jean at Dene House. Jim was one of the first men to be employed at Ellington Colliery in 1910, when he transferred from Linton.

Hay raking at home farm, 1947. Seated is Cynthia Proctor and Norman Little with Billy French and horse, Denny.

The corn harvest almost over at home farm, *circa* 1952. Little Jim Beattie stands with dad Eddie, then unknown, George Cleghorn, Alan Rochester, Bob Charlton and Mr Charlton.

Trying out the horse's new shoes at Dene House are: Davey Crawford and Dave Hindmarsh. Standing, left to right: Ray Shields, Joe Blake, George Hume and Colin Farrier.

The dairy girls of East Moor, *circa* 1950s. Standing, left to right: Lena Tulloch, Lily Mather, Kathy Scott, Nellie Nicholson, Jean Carr. Front: Joyce Brown, Nancy Bell, Joan Bell.

Hugh Crawford forging the front shoe of a Clydesdale at Dene House in the 1950s.

Shops

As its name suggests, Market Square was intended to be the centre of the village. The 1926 strike delayed all plans to extend the village east to Lyneburn and eventually this scheme was shelved. This is where the main shopping area was sited. Ashington Coal Company did not allow any traders at the south side. Only once, when there was war damage to Wilkinson's shop in 1941 are there records of the use of a house in Ingelby Terrace for trading. Jane Miles worked at Wilkinson's and at Pearson's stores after the war years.

Right: Jane Miles in the back shop of Wilkinson's in 1924. She is still hale and hearty at the grand old age of 94. She served in Wilkinson's and Pearson's stores from 1924-66 and in a house in Ingelby Terrace after a landmine destroyed Wilkinson's in 1941. Names of the past traders in West Market Street included: Smails – butchers, Moyes – fish and chips, Pearson's – grocer, Elliot – bakers, Charlton's – chemist, Proudlock – bakers, Bardon – ice-cream, Mary Stafford – confectionery. Hairdressers included: Esther Oliver, Elsie Nichol and, present day, Sharon's. In Albion Terrace there was Chrisp's newsagents, also used as a bank in the early years, Graham's baker, Co-op fruit and veg and bakery, Wilson Cochrane, Barber Easton – newsagent, Clavering Post Office, Leonard Post Office, Archibold – grocer and Robinson – grocer. A betting shop was also used adjacent Stafford's newsagents. Basil Morris repaired books and shoes and prior to this the Fosters traded. Mr & Mrs Patrick, grocers, traded near to the West Bridge.

West Market Street looking north, *circa* 1940s.

Jimmy Smail opened his shop in 1925 and was renowned for his quality of meat through the years. The staff in 1958 included: John Easton, Ian Patterson, Bill Smail, Jim Anderson and Irene Smail.

A rare picture of Moyes fish shop in 1928 on the West Green with Mr Hogg in foreground.

The first houses can be seen being built in Market Square, in the background of this photograph, *circa* 1947. Here are the three girls who worked in Mary Stafford's shop: Lilly Stafford, Rosemary Habberjam and Ella Foster.

Of the original occupants of Lynemouth shops only the Co-op remain as tenants. The others have changed hands many times since 1925. There are less premises trading now and the Lynemouth population is at its lowest since 1941. This is essentially due to the demise of the coal industry. Eleanor Tuck remembers:

'The Co-op in Lynemouth was a branch of Ashington Industrial Co-op situated in West Market Street, the main shopping area in Lynemouth, five shops, a grocery (the only Co-op shop now) greengrocers, butchers, drapery and hardware (upstairs from the drapery).

There were two other small shops in Albion Terrace, a grocery and a green grocery department. The hardware department opened in 1949. In 1956 when I came to work there it was a regular customers trade. Most people were members with a store check book and check number. I still remember my mother's number – 287.

Dividend was paid on purchases, every size months – usually in March and September. In the hardware and drapery, customers could have goods on credit and pay at the end of the half year, ie March and September. For about two weeks no credit was given at the end and the beginning of half year, for stock taking and new stock to arrive.

Four of the Co-op lasses of the 1950s outside the store: Mary Clancey, Eleanor Weddell, Mary Oliver and Jean Longstaff.

One day, a man asked me when did the Baltic open. I was rather puzzled at what he meant until he explained his wife wanted some goods on tick (credit).

The grocery department delivered weekly orders to customers, first by horse and cart and then by small van. The delivery man, Jack Rowell, was very helpful and delivered small parcels for customers – from hardware and drapery, along with weekly groceries.

Best selling hardware goods were wallpaper, paint, brushes, brooms, shovels, roofing felt and nails for garden sheds, carbide for miner's lamps, thermos flasks, alarm clocks and crockery. When the greengrocers closed down, the shop stood empty for a while then it was refurbished and the hardware department was moved into it. When the North Eastern Co-op was formed, hardware and drapery was merged into one department known as the non-food dept, until its closure in 1982.'

Woodhorn Mill

The present mill, which is at the eastern entrance to Alcan's Aluminium Smelter, was built in 1846 by Robert Hindhaugh. It stands on the site of a former wooden mill which was burned down. Robert Hindhaugh had three daughters and one son. One day, one of his daughters took her father's lunch, and walked out on to the loading gantry. Her long skirt was blown by the wind and caught in the sails, she was flung into a field and died of her injuries. The Hindhaugh family were devastated by this tragedy and Robert never worked the mill again. Fate struck again in the 1970s when a young lad died while climbing the mill. Before the advent of the giant Aluminium Smelter, Woodhorn Mill was a landmark, situated on a sandstone knoll and a mark to navigate by for local fishermen. To the people of Lynemouth it was a reassuring figure that meant that home was near, just at the end of the mill road. The sails have gone, but fortunately Alcan played a large part in retaining this historical building. The entrance has been sealed to protect it from vandals and windows added to enhance its appearance.

Left: The woman and child stand at the end of a track which ran behind the mill and on to Lynemouth. A popular walk with villagers.

Below: The Mill as it looks today.

New Kids On The Block

With 1972 came the completion of the building of the giant Alcan UK Aluminium Smelter and coal-fired power station. Situated one mile to the south east of Lynemouth, it provided a welcome boost to the local economy and gave stability to the declining pits in the area. Most of the original commissioning crew came from Canada, the company's headquarters at Montreal. They were French Canadians and were housed in Ashington. They integrated fairly well and were impressed by the Geordies' ability to learn new skills. In return they received a sense of humour and a fresh outlook on life from our people. The smelter and power station's 200 foot high chimneys dominate the skyline. Visible for miles from every point of the compass, The sheer scale of the complex has placed Lynemouth well and truly on the map. Thus for the first time since the early 1900s, when Ellington Colliery commenced operations, a new brand of industry was introduced to Lynemouth. The Government welcomed the smelter, as it was in an area where mining was in decline. It gave employment to ex-miners and would boost the local economy in a deprived area.

The smelter and power station were built simultaneously as was the ship unloading facility (SUF) at Blyth. The late delivery of structural steel, labour troubles and bad weather meant that the plant did not go into full production until the spring of 1972 instead of early 1971.

An aerial view, looking north, of the smelter, power station and coal preparation plant.

The Carbon Plant – Manufactures carbon anodes used in the electrolytic process.

The Casting Plant – Converts the whole of the smelter output into rolling ingots and despatched to customers by rail, sea and air. Products produced include road signs, building materials, packaging, foil, etc.

The Potrooms – Molten metal is siphoned from pre-bake pots into crucibles, each pot yields about one ton of aluminium a day.

SECTION TWO

LEISURE

Mrs Wallace, and neighbour, with Jean, Isobel and Nellie Hogg at Lynemouth beach with Strawberry Hill to the right, *circa* 1930. Behind the girls, where once stood superb sand dunes, is now the site of the Alcan Power Station.

Was There Ever A Strawberry Hill?

Yes, there certainly was, but to the younger generation of Lynemouth residents, Strawberry Hill is a place that they will only have heard mentioned by family or friends. Situated 200 yards from the mouth of the River Lyne on its north side, it boasted fine sand dunes to the south, east and north. Its top was a mass of wild strawberries, harebells, and thyme which thrived in the free draining sandy soil.

Lynemouth then had its own special recreational facility on its doorstep. Villagers could picnic, bathe and camp in the years leading up to the 1950s. The correct name for the hill, as depicted on early references and maps is Linmouth Hill, but to the local people it was affectionately known as Strawberry Hill.

In the General Strike of 1926 it began to rival Newbiggin as a seaside resort. Day-trippers were transported by charabanc to this idyllic little spot from the inland towns.

From the 1930s, when Ashington Coal Company created railway sidings, the hill was steadily disappearing. By the 1950s colliery waste tipping was in full flow and had a huge impact on the area, Strawberry Hill vanished beneath a black spoil heap.

A gypsy site now exists in its place and is under the Jurisdiction of Morpeth County Council. The tipping of colliery waste is necessary for the future of Ellington Combine. The only alternative to this is the threat of opencast mining and subsequent tipping at nearby Windmill Hill. This area is to be reclaimed in the near future. Whatever occurs in future years, one fact emerges, there will never be a Strawberry Hill as the village knew in the early years.

A happy group of Lynemouth folk on top of Strawberry Hill in 1938 – the first ever pit holidays. Back: Mrs Gallon, Muriel Thompson, Dick Tunney, Tommy Thompson and Bob Thompson. Middle: Mrs Taylor, Jean Taylor, Mrs Turnbull, Mrs Tunney, Audrey Rainbow, Mamie Thompson, Winnie Thompson and Isobel Thompson. Front: Bob Laws, Sid Swinhoe and Denis Swinhoe.

Where Have All The Summers Gone

Extracts from Mary Preston's Poem

Where have all the summers gone
The ones we used to know
When every day was sunny and bright
And filled with things for our delight
A fishing net, pail and spade
Arrangements for a picnic made
Then the word was sent around
To Aunty Violet, Mrs Brown
Uncles Bob, Will and Joe
And cousins and friends who would like to go

At Woodhorn we passed the Old Grey Mill
Standing proud upon a hill
A little further round the turn,
We took the path down to Lyne Burn,
Look there's dunes, white sand and sea
No need for money, everything's free.

While parents were busy we'd time to kill
We picked the fruit on Strawberry Hill
No better sandwiches tasted
Not a crumb of food was ever wasted

Midday sun shone at its best
Gran and Grandad have gone for a rest
Tug O war for the men, rounders for all
A prize for the best sand castle standing so tall

Now where have all the Summers gone
I think that you will find
That they are where they'll always be
Forever in our mind.

The beach as it looks now looking south towards Lynemouth's Alcan Power Station and smelter with Lynemouth Coal Preparation Plant in the centre.

The River Lyne

The river is tidal, and therefore silt and industrial waste from nearby Ellington Colliery can be seen to be deposited at a distance from the river mouth.

Looking west at the tidal flats from the coast bridge, *circa* 1948. The course of the river was diverted slightly in 1967, with the construction of Lynemouth Colliery's new Bewick Drift. This occurred half a mile inland from its outlet. The picture changes at this point, as the Lyne incorporates areas of reedbeds and damp places which are an attraction for waterfowl.

Right: The Lyne today as it flows beneath the Bewick belt drift. Pollution has been a problem with Ashington Colliery washery waste entering the burn at Hayden Letch in Ellington Dene. In the 1960s certain toxic pesticides were used by farmers. The residue from these chemicals flowed into the Lyne and much of the river was devoid of any life form. Now that this practice has ceased, the result is a steady recovery. Herons can be seen stalking eels and frogs, kingfishers hunt daily and trout inhabit the upper reaches.

Wild mink, originally escapees from captivity are a real threat to the river bank taking waterfowl eggs and the fast disappearing water vole. In 1998 a survey conducted by the Northumberland Wildlife Trust of all the rivers in the county, showed that otters had not been observed to have colonised the Lyne. However local knowledge suggests that they have, whether they stay to breed, only time will tell. It would appear that the burn is returning to its glory years of pre-1960.

Kingfishers

Where reedy Lyne runs slow and wide,
From the confines of my makeshift hide,
I chanced to see the King of Kings
Slip by on multi-coloured wings.

At the ivied bridge, a sight so rare,
He hovered silent in the air,
Like a giant hummingbird was he,
His rainbow spectrum I could see.

Orange green and hectic red,
With a speckled crest upon his head,
His sky blue rump and chestnut thighs
A snow white patch neath his coal
black eyes.

Still I lay, lest he should see
A stranger close by willow tree,

Oh how I wished that I could be
As bright and masterful as he.

He chose to perch on alder bare
Above the clear cool river there,
I wondered if he had paused to rest,
His spear like beak on burnished breast.

But no, he called three times soft and low,
As if to say, where are you, its time to go,
And from the cover of the pump house wall
An answer to his mating call.

How fortunate was I to see,
Two kingfishers on alder tree,
In half light fly off to greet
Springtime to their mile long beat.

Neil Taylor

Lynemouth And Ellington Dene

For two miles, from Ellington Bridge to the west to the tidal flats to the east, the river Lyne meanders between steep banks clothed with shrubs and high rise trees. The Dene provides a natural shelter belt protecting Lynemouth from the north and west. The area from Sea View to Lyne Terrace on the south side of the river is owned by the parish council and walks have been created here.

Looking east at the landscaped area today. To the north this is under the control of mining operator R.J. Budge, it is designated semi-ancient woodland. North to Chugdon Wood is the southern limit of the proposed opencast operation of Windmill Hill. This parcel of woodland was keepered by Ashington Coal Company and later by the National Coal Board.

From the second bridge, George Hume stands in front of conifers which are now 40 foot high, *circa* 1948.

Alan Simpson remembers:

'In the 1930s the village brass band played on Sunday evenings in the summer glade, just to the left of the first bridge over the river Lyne. Labour Party speakers would then voice their opinions and policies, among these was Jimmy Maxton easily recognised by his long flowing hair. The people of the village would sit on the grassy bank which formed a natural arena. The congregation would be given strength from the meetings, at a time when the miners were receiving a mere pittance for their slave labour in the privately owned pits. There was a ford here which crossed the river, and a road which rose steeply past Lynemouth Allotments, then on to a lonnen which ran to the south of Lynemouth Welfare and continued as a track to its meeting with the Windmill at Woodhorn.'

Alan Simpson, aged three, on stepping stones at the ford, *circa* 1925.

SPORT

Jack Fairfax giving the bowling green a final
cut, it was always in perfect condition,
circa 1940.

Lynemouth Welfare grounds and sports pavilion were in use from 1924. However, it was on the 9th May 1925 that the official opening was performed by Ashington Coal Company's Managing Director Ridley Warham. 'Lucky Lynemouth' was the opinion of the guests at the opening ceremony. Designed by W. Cookson, the coal company's surveyor, it was proposed to cater for all the sporting needs of the people who would eventually inhabit the pit village. The pavilion housed a tea room, committee room dressing rooms, ante rooms and bathing areas. There was a specially equipped kitchen, electric lighting and central heating. The grounds covered fourteen acres and comprised of a cricket oval, a football pitch with space for another, five grass tennis courts, bowling green and space for putting and croquet. There were access paths, areas of shrubs and hedges with seats placed in strategic places. However, it was not a free handout to the miners as two pence a week was deducted from their pay to finance Ashington Coal Company's Welfare scheme. In addition a half penny a ton was levied on the cost of coal. Ashington Coal Company had followed the lead of soap manufacturer Lord Leverhulme and Rowntree the chocolate maker in providing housing and recreation facilities for its workers. From 1924 a Children's Gala was allowed the use of the grounds, a venue still in existence to this day. From 1925 Lynemouth and Ellington band met and practised there, parish council meetings and all sports functions were held in the pavilion. Lynemouth Methodists had meetings prior to 1927.

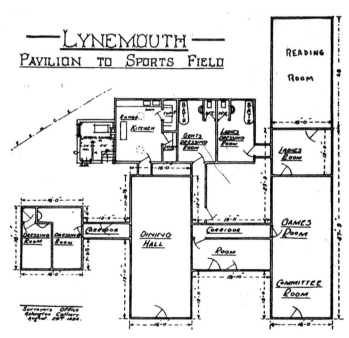

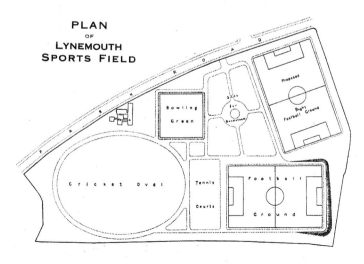

PLAN
OF
LYNEMOUTH
SPORTS FIELD

Always well supported, this is the Gala of 1957. Front left is Brenda Chapman with bike and Sandra Harding pushing her pram. Mrs Tunn is back right.

The village entered teams in all sports, many fine teams have used the Welfare facilities. Cricket is once again played on the oval after an absence of many years. Football is healthy with a strong emphasis on Sunday soccer. The Welfare is now under the control of Castle Morpeth Council, who employ a groundsman to oversee the facilities. The old pavilion has gone now, replaced by a more modern building, as has the wooden bowling hut. Bowls are again played at Lynemouth after a period of rest due to problems with the playing surface.

One evening, during the bandsmen's interval, one of their members decided to join a group of footballers including myself doing some serious training for a weekend cup match. We used a spring board, vaulted a box, and then a forward roll. Our bandsman friend hit the spring board, cleared the box, missed the mat on the other side and head butted the outside door. We had never seen a jump like that, and as he lay moaning we fell about laughing, and then carried the bouncing bandsman back to the bandroom. He lay on a table to recover while the band played on. He eventually came to but he never appeared again in the exercise hall to the dismay of all the football team, who wanted a repeat performance.

The Welfare Groundsman

John (Jack) Fairfax joined the Northumberland Fusiliers aged 19 years and with the Machine Gun Corp took part in some of the bloodiest battles of the First World War. After this he returned to Ashington and became a banksman for the Bothal Pit. A love for the outdoor life led Jack to apply for the new position of groundsman at Ashington Coal Companies New Hirst Welfare Park.

Therefore, along with Mr George Murdie, Mr A. Watson and Mr G. Clementson he became among the first men in the country to be employed full-time on a miners' welfare scheme of this kind. This was in 1921 and Jack remained based there including short visits to Linton Welfare for 11 years. He then took up the position as Welfare Groundsman at Lynemouth in 1932, and lived at 18 Jersey Square in the village. He was at this time also doing duties at Lynemouth Picture Hall.

Jack was a proud man, maybe a trait he acquired from his war service. There was no doubt as to who was in charge. The grounds were meticulously maintained, and the machines treated lovingly. Any sporting effects had to be returned in good condition, and Jack became more than a groundsman, being secretary of many indoor and outdoor activities. His pride and joy were the tennis courts, no-one was allowed in the area without the proper footwear. Sunday was rest day in the early years, the Welfare gates were locked and no sports were allowed. But on a Sunday afternoon boys being boys, would gather on the football pitch and all ages would engage in a free for all football match. We knew at some stage it would be stopped. Jack played a war game, appearing from nowhere and boys would scatter in all directions, and so it continued the following Sunday, a game never won or lost. Jack Fairfax was held in great esteem by the many people who used the Welfare facilities.

Jack retired in February 1964, after giving 42 years service to the Welfare organisation, 30 years of these at Lynemouth. A presentation at the Hirst Welfare Pavilion was attended by the Welfare staff, wives and friends. Jack was presented with a chiming clock by his friend and colleague Mr G.L. Murdie.

George Murdie on the left presenting Jack with his chiming clock on his retirement.

Harry Lister

The 1930s saw a great number of hungry hard fighters in the boxing ring. Amongst them came the fighting men of Lynemouth. The O'Keefe's family had a good quartet of fighters, Eddie, Tommy, Pat and Sexton, all quality fighters. Another useful fighter was Eddie Hanson but quite a following of boxing from that era will agree came one man with real outstanding fighting qualities – Harry Lister.

Harry was born in 1916 into a family of giants, Harry grew to 6' 2" and weighed 14 stone at his best fighting weight. He had two brothers even taller, the dwarf of the family at 6' 0" was his father.

Harry left the coal mining employment in 1935 when he was 19 years old to follow a career in boxing. His southpaw stance proved quite an attraction for the spectators. He scored plenty of points with his right lead and did a lot of damage with his left. Lister had a total of 58 fights, lost 4, drew 1 and one no-contest – a very impressive record especially when you find out Harry sometimes had 3 and 4 fights in a month.

Quite a few of Harry's fights were local but he also travelled to Scotland, Wales and Ireland in his quest for recognition, beating the area and national champions in the process of doing this. A lot of ringside experts called him a real good prospect with his southpaw stance proving so awkward opponents were scared of meeting him. Max Baer once said to him: 'Change your stance son and you'll get plenty of fights.' But Harry did not listen and continued to win a lot of fights by knockouts. Soon promoters started to take notice, people were saying: 'What a novelty a heavyweight southpaw let's have a look at him.' Soon he was able to book more fights than he could fulfil.

Harry Lister at 21, the most promising heavyweight in Britain. Sadly Harry died at the age of 57.

Bill Foster remembers:

Harry Lister trained often at the Lynemouth Institute, upstairs where the leek show is now held. He could be heard thumping his hammer left hand into his unfortunate sparring partners, and often one would be knocked clean through the swing doors.

It must be noted that Harry returned to work in the pit during the war years and only took the 1945 fight as a last minute substitute after being out of action for five years. The fight was stopped, but Harry had never been knocked out in any of his fights. He had in those five wonderful years knocked out or stopped at least 30 of his opponents. There are some of the old boxing fraternity who thought Harry could have beaten Jack London for the Northern Area Championship and that may well be true, we will never know, but Jack London was a fine boxer in his own right.

The KO O'Keefes

Luther O'Keefe began work in the pits at 12 years of age and retired when he was 72. A tough man he produced six diamonds in the boxing ring. Of the fighting O'Keefes, Mattie, John and Eddie fought with distinction, while Tommy, Pat and Sexton made a living in the top bracket during the 1930s. They were hard times then, it often meant working a shift underground and then a bruising battle in the ring for the lads. One of the greatest middleweight fights ever seen in the north east was Pat's encounter with hard hitting local lad Andy McLaughlin in the Princess Ballroom, Ashington in 1936 which Pat won on points. Tommy became the official pitmen's lightweight champion in 1934 when defeating vastly experienced Jack Dibbs in a contest which carried a sidestake of £10, a nest egg at that time. The Second World War saw Sexton and Tommy in service. Tommy in the thick of infantry action in North Africa, Sicily and Italy. After demobilisation Tommy returned to Lynemouth Colliery until retirement. Of the punch proud brothers only Tommy survives and at almost 86 years old is still as game as he was those many years ago when he fought for a living.

In the army and still boxing, Corporal Tommy O'Keefe (left) in a contest with Lieutenant Murray at Gamdale Camp in 1939.

Versatility

There is an old saying which originated in the north east pit villages, that if a Football League team was short of a player, then all that was needed was a shout down the nearest mine shaft. Such was the interest and talent on the local soccer scene.

One person who was more than able was Lynemouth footballer John (Jacky) Herron, undoubtedly the most versatile player ever to originate from the village. At Lynemouth School his potential was seen by sports master Bob Young, who included Jack then aged eleven in the U-15 team.

At 14 years of age he gained county honours for Northumberland at centre half, appearing with Bobby Charlton against Durham in 1952. His performance was magnificent as he snuffed out the challenge of the Durham and England centre forward. Further county honours followed, it was then that Football League teams took notice of the tall classy youngster.

After leaving school in 1953, Jack followed in his father's footsteps and began work at nearby Ellington Colliery. Evenings and Saturdays he played football for Newcastle United Juniors for two seasons, before ending his junior career at Lynemouth. In 1956 Jack joined Amble FC who operated in the Northern Alliance League.

Playing at centre half, he also had a passion for attacking play. Standing six foot tall and weighing 12 stone he was not easily knocked off the ball. Noting

Jacky is seen here (centre middle) aged eleven in the Lynemouth School senior team in 1949-50.

Jack's fondness for going forward, Amble manager, John Armstrong, moved him to centre forward. Jack proceeded to score 18 goals in 8 games, which attracted the attention of 10 Football League clubs, including Newcastle and Sunderland.

He could strike a dead or moving ball with either foot, possessed great control and was an excellent header of a ball. Added to this was his ability to defend or attack, and voice his opinions in no uncertain terms. It was John Armstrong who persuaded Jack to sign semi-professional forms for Leeds United. John had secured a deal with manager of Leeds, Raich Carter, and Amble FC received £250 for the signing on. This was in 1956 but Jack's job at Ellington Colliery was secured.

His first match for Leeds reserve team saw him score against the Chesterfield keeper, the great Gordon Banks. In the following weeks he averaged a goal per game and being groomed at that time by the Leeds United legend, John Charles. Ashington lad Jack Charlton was then centre half in the same team. However, Herron was not settled with Leeds United, he wanted to play football and retain his job at the pit. Gateshead FC heard this news and offered him a contract on semi-professional terms in 1957. He accepted and played in most positions in attack for four years, before converting to defence and captaining the side for six years. He was considered by the Leeds coach Ivor Powell to be the best young prospect football had produced for many years. How good in the top flight, we will never know. His twilight years in football were spent with Ashington under managers Davey Davidson and Ken Prior.

His versatility does not end there, for Jack was a crucial member of Bomarsund Welfare's Cricket team that won the Haig National Village Trophy in 1974, a tremendous feat for a Geordie side.

A Lynemouth cricket team from the 1930s, not many of these lads around today. Back: Tom Johnson, Stan Levison, Andy Brotherton, Tom Laidler, Tom Gibbons, George Conway and Jack Fairfax. Front: Jim Simpson, Len Noctor, Chris Taylor, Jack Foster, Bill Davison and Albert Tait. Forefront: Fred Harding.

A Lifetime In Football
by Malcolm Musgrove

I attended Lynemouth school from 1938-44 then passed a scholarship examination to attend Morpeth Grammar School from 1944-49. After leaving school my first job was as a wages clerk in the Lynemouth Colliery office under chief cashier Mr John McCoy.

Whilst at the Grammar School I played rugby on a Saturday morning for the school and football for Lynemouth juniors in the afternoon, and also played cricket for both my village and school teams.

In 1951 at the age of eighteen I was called up to do my National Service in the RAF for two years, and while in the RAF I was stationed in Aberdeen. On leave at Lynemouth I was 'spotted' playing football for the village team by a Londoner working in the area. He got me a trial at West Ham which went well and I was invited to sign professional forms on my demob from the RAF in November 1953. After nine happy years at West Ham I met my wife Jean during this time and we were married in 1957.

After West Ham came a move to Leyton Orient for four years before moving on to the coaching side of the game with Charlton Athletic who were managed by former Newcastle United player Bob Stokoe.

In 1967 I moved to Aston Villa to join Tommy Cummings another Geordie who had played for Burnley. Then came a move from Aston Villa to Leicester City as chief coach under manager Frank O'Farrell where our success included promotion to the First Division and an FA Cup Final against Manchester City. Frank took over at Manchester United and he invited me to be his assistant which I gladly accepted. Success eluded us at Old Trafford and after a short stay came a move to Torquay United to take over as manager from 1973-76. I was then in Connecticut and Chicago in the North America Soccer League which had players of the calibre of Pele and Cruyff playing for New York and Los Angeles.

After my return to England I took a job with Exeter City as a coach under manager Brian Godfrey. While with Exeter, I qualified as a sports physiotherapist and accepted a position with the Quatar National team in the Arabian Gulf. After returning to England, after one year abroad, I joined Plymouth Argyle and stayed for seven years before an old West Ham playing mate, John Bond, invited me to join him at Shrewsbury Town. I stayed at

Shrewsbury until my retirement last year. I have many happy memories of Lynemouth village and of the people who came to find work in the coal mines.

Malcolm is pictured here (bottom right) in a fine West Ham side, *circa* 1957/58. Second left at the back is Geoff Hurst, 5th back is John Bond and then Bobby Moore.

Lynemouth Welfare Booth Cup Winners, *circa* 1942. Back: Matty McSparron, Walter Brown, Bob McLean, and Jack Spedding. Middle: Jack Mather, Jim Jeffries, Jack Foster, Jim Tomlin, Andy Brotherton, Tommy Gibbons and Jack Fairfax. Front: Bill Davison, Joe Heard and Jack Waddell.

Lynemouth Dynamoes Ladies Football team, 1949-50. The ladies formed a team to raise funds for the local men's soccer team and for charity. Back: Bella Cowan, Esther Oliver, Kathleen Jenkins, Jean Conway, Florrie Dixon, Florrie Dunning and Sylvia Mitcheson. Front: Mona Taylor, Betty Jenkins, Joan Hollanby, Sadie Mitcheson, Ella Taylor and A. Murray.

Lynemouth Cricket 2nd Team, 1951. Back: Harry Shears, Alan Tweddle, Alf Shepherd, and H. Turnbull. Middle: D. Partis, Tom Lister, Eddie Straker, Sid Stowe and J. Willis. Front: George Sharp, Terry Woolers. The little girl in the centre is Jean Sharp and on the right Olive Sharp, the girls travelled with dad George to all his cricket venues. The girl on the left is Helen Willis.

The Welfare side are seen wearing the old style lace strips, *circa* 1949. Back: Jackie Spratt, Cliff Waldock, George Taylor, Brian Waugh, Jim Hindmarsh, Bobby Orr, Jimmy Stephens. Front: Bob Thompson, unknown, George Shepherd, Bill Tully, Dick Spratt, Jackie Potter, Andy Hay.

Always a hard team to beat, this side had players of county standard with Jim Simpson and Bob Snowball, *circa* 1953. Winners of the Alnwick and District League, Knockout Cup and the Ravensworth Bowl. Back: Ed Straker, Tom Lister, Jim Brown, Jack Foster, Andy Brotherton, Ray Poxton and Alan Simpson. Front: Eric Murray, Jim Simpson, Alec Anderson, Bob Snowball, Tom Laidler and Bill Robinson.

The grins on the faces of Lynemouth Cricket team of 1962 tell a story. In the final of the Ashington knockout cup versus Linton they decided to have their photograph taken with the trophy before the game! Thankfully they won. Back: Gordon Walker, Bill Waddell, Alan Youngs, Stan Levison, Bob Clyde, Jackie Herron and Alf Shepherd. Front: Steve Mavin, Alan Peart, Tom Lister, Eric Murray and Andy Johnson.

Presentation night for players and officials at Harmonic Hall in 1952 representing Lynemouth Juniors FC. Back: Jim Batey, T. Medlen, Jim Green, Joe Hogg and Henry Cleverley. Middle: Tom Lister, Matty Davison, Bill Cleverley, Alan Tweddle, Kelly, Jim Stephens. Front: Neil Kelly and Gordon Crawford.

Lots of the local lads played cricket as well as football. This Lynemouth junior side of 1960 was coached by Alec Anderson. Rear: Alec Anderson. Back: Arthur Hanson, Henry Adamson, Owen Taylor, Jim Adamson, Watson Cowton, George Adamson and Jim McLeod. Front: Bob Huntley, Arthur Kidd, Jim Campbell and Barry Harding.

Ladies football was revived in 1972. Here are stalwart defenders Pat Wall, Pat Knowles and Irene Robson seeing off an opponent's attack, while keeper Margaret Lister stands guard.

These lads represented Lynemouth in the Northern Alliance League when as many as a thousand people would attend the home matches, *circa* 1952. Back: J. Hindmarsh, John Willis, Ivan Armstrong, Fred Weddell, Jim Hindmarsh, unknown. Front: G. Nichol, T. Johnson, R. Brewis, J. Dowson and Alan Bell.

SCHOOLDAYS

Rhythm and balance in the schoolyard, *circa* 1926. The old POW hut is seen in the background and was used as a classroom prior to 1926.

Lynemouth School

The urgent need for a school to cater for the educational requirements of the children in an expanding mining village was well documented in 1924-1925 Parish records. Most of the pupils prior to the opening of new Lynemouth school on 3rd May 1926 travelled to Ellington or Ashington. However there was a report of wooden huts on the site as early as 1924 which served older children for a short while.

Lynemouth First School, save for hi-tech security, little has changed. Mr Herron, the Ellington headmaster, transferred to the new Lynemouth facility on its opening and was not sorry to leave the primitive facilities behind. Instead of a complex of old dimly lit huts with little heating or lighting, Lynemouth's new brick purpose built school contained large warm classrooms, meeting hall, play areas and modern toilet blocks. Ex-army huts were also used as the number of children at that time was 563. The east and west wings of Lynemouth Methodist Chapel have been utilised at certain stages to house any overflow of pupils from the school, unfortunately the opening of the new school coincided with the first day of the 1926 General Strike. Nevertheless 35,327 dinners were provided free of charge to the youngsters during its ten month duration.

In May 1986 the school celebrated its diamond jubilee. Lynemouth was then a first school with a total of 175 pupils. Over 200 former staff and pupils were invited and attended an open day and concert. A display of old photographs and memorabilia were shown, and the classrooms transformed into replicas of the 1920s with old fashioned desks and inkwells. The concert included music from Ellington Colliery Band and Ashington YMCA Gleemen. Headmaster Mr Rogers also opened the school to members of the public in the afternoon and evening. The buildings remain much the same, save for the demolition of the air-raid shelters and the former canteen to the north of the school. The main school's corridor arches have been sealed and glazed which gives a much warmer feel to the classrooms. The only addition to the hall area, a hi-tech kitchen to provide school meals. There is a sense of pride in the smart blue sweatered youngsters and this is a reflection on the capabilities of the teaching staff who give more than their allotted time to the children.

A Friends of the School organisation meets monthly and provides various fund raising events to subsidise the school budget. The young people of Lynemouth will have every opportunity to advance their education under the present system.

The first teaching staff. Back: unknown, unknown, Minnie Dunn, unknown, John Jackson, Edith Foster. Front: Mr Reekie, unknown, Mr Herron, unknown, Mr Wash and Scamp. Edith Foster transferred from Ellington School in 1926, her father owned a Boot and Shoe Shop in Albion Terrace.

The School Netball Team of 1936-37. Back: Mary Huntley, Vera Brown, Betty Spowart, Esther Oliver. Front: Betty Moore, Iris Musgrove, Etty Cram – note in the background Dr Skene's surgery on the right, the chapel centre and police house left. The building of the Dalton Avenue council houses came post-war.

In the back row, third right is Bill Sharp, George Sharp is far right, third row and Bill Foster second left, front row.

Lynemouth School Staff, 1948. Back: Mr Blair, Miss Neave, Mr Pyle and Mr Gotts. Middle: Miss Dodds, Mrs Robertson, Mrs Bird, Mrs Nixon, Miss Snowdon and Mrs Lillico. Front: Mr Youngs, Miss Foster, Mr Graham (Head), Miss Rhodes and Mr Reekie.

School Senior Football Team, *circa* 1948-49. Back: Mr Jackson, Alan Reed, J. Blake, Ron Dunning, Tom Lister, Alf Shepherd, John Johnson and Mr Youngs. Front: George Hanson, Tom Sweet, Bob Cook, Gordon Crawford and Jos Hanson.

Walter Brown taking his turn at the skittles in the School Hall, *circa* 1928.

Lynemouth Rose Queen was held as part of the old Ashington Carnival, which raised funds for the Ashington Coal Company's Hospital. These bonny lasses are pictured outside the hospital, *circa* 1931. Back row, left to right: Brenda Hedley, Jennie Summers, Nancy McLean, Elsie Medlen, Betty Chrisp, Jean Hogg. Middle: Nellie Hogg, Dulcie Anderson, Kitty Wollers, Annie McQuillan, Rose Queen (name unknown), Betty Spowart, Connie Rickaby, Hazel Graham. Front: C. Dobson, Eva Hall, Noreen Hedley, Eva Teasdale.

One of the first stage productions was *Princess Juju, circa* 1935. Third right of the boys is Jim Simpson and fourth Tom Morris.

Lynemouth County Primary School Football - any of these lads still around will now be well into their seventies. Back: Isaac Grint, Stan Tilley, Ivan Armstrong, Fred Cairns, Frank Lister. Middle: Bill Kidd, E. Locker, Tom Foster, Matty Richardson. Front: George Taylor, R. Murray, Ernie Taylor.

The play was *Mother Goose*, the scenery created by Mr Cessford the art teacher who is pictured third left in second front row. Second left is Audrey Stimpson the popular music teacher, *circa* 1955. Sadly Audrey died recently after a long and successful career in music circles.

Miss Rhodes class of school leavers in 1949. Back: Don Gowland, Mary Mavin, Jim Chapman, unknown, unknown, Rosemary Habberjam. Seated: John Johnson, Audrey Shields, Joe Patterson, Norma Thompson and Bob Batey. Front: Melvyn Neil.

Lynemouth School Pantomime, 1954. Back: Marion Moulding, Sylvia
Thompson, Ann Purdy, Lynn Lewins, June Taylor, Norma Strachan, Sylvia
Hanson, Pat Ascot, Ada Hindmarsh, Alice Pollard. Second back: unknown,
Winnifed Stafford, Isobel Strachan, Margaret Teasdale, Dorothy Clark, Audrey
Penman, unknown, Bill Gray. Third back: Davey Crawford, Brian Davison,
Tucker Ewart, Kathy Woollet, Stella Dunning, John Raine, Lily Mather, Rose
Taylor, Gerry McGee. Fourth row: Bob Weddell, Alan Peart, Winnie Cowton,
Billy Chatt, Stella Hanson, Jean Mack, Cynthia Hanson, Lothar Muller, Brian
Lonsdale, unknown, Les Ions. Front: Joe Blake, Ann Houlison, Ann Lockyer,
Margaret Mead, Heather Marsh, Jakey Turnbull and Lynn Lewins.

The last year infants 2 class, *circa* 1950. These youngsters will be well into
their fifties now.

Lynemouth School Junior Team. There was no school bus in those days to travel to away games, it was all done by local transport, often resulting in matches being delayed awaiting the away side. Back: Colin Farrier, Jim Graham, Neil Taylor, George Stewart, Alan Dickinson and Richard Crewe. Front: Clarry Green, George Heard, George Hume, Ray Hindmarsh and Jimmy Conway.

These three local girls made up the Gala Queen and her attendants, and for once they had good weather to celebrate the event, *circa* 1953. Left to right: Cynthia Hanson, Irene Smail (Gala Queen) and Eva Dickinson.

Class 10 - Miss Duxfield's girls of 1949. Middle: unknown, Brenda Thompson, Margaret Woolage, Mary Foster, Jean Sharp, Mary Pollard, Gloria Mears and Janet Ewart. Front: Brenda C. Thompson, Mary Hogg, Carol Rhodes, Ann Pickering, Elsie Davison and Ann Simpson

The School Pantomime of 1949 includes the two senior class pupils.

This is a picture of the last year infants, *circa* 1950. The arches at the rear have now been sealed and glazed.

The class of 1949 shows Miss Dodd's girls. Back: unknown, unknown, unknown, Betty Hume. Middle: Ann Templey, Maureen Mathews, Joyce Tweddle, Gwen Nicholson, Olga Adamson, Marion Redshaw, Audrey Penman, Doreen Hanson. Front: Joan Bone, Margaret Nicholson, Sheila Heard, Joan Gargett and Margaret Bone.

The senior 2 class of 1950.

Miss Dodd's boys of 1949. Back: Ivan Lister, unknown, John Mathews, Ted Dixon, Joe Pollard, Keith Lister and Sid Meredith. Middle: Henry Cleverley, Ian Lunn, David Price, Maurice Hanson, Brian Hume and Robert Moffatt. Front: unknown, Eric Liddell, J. Teasdale, Brian Sweet, Ted Cooper and Jim Bergfeld

The present day teaching and auxiliary staff. Lynemouth now a First School includes a Nursery Section. Back: Mrs H. Gray, Mrs H. Macdonald, Mrs C. Dodds, Mrs G. Cowie, Mrs F. Smith, Miss W. Phillips, Mrs P. Newcombe and Miss Louise Brown. Front: Mrs F. Smith, Mrs E. Dunn, Mr B. Johnson (Headteacher) Mrs J. Simpson (Deputy Head) and Mrs P. Lumsdon.

Headteachers

Mr Herron 1926-1940

Mr Graham 1940-1967

Mr Perris 1967-1981

Mrs Hall 1981-1984

Mr Rodgers 1984-1997

Mrs Simpson 1997-1998

Mr Johnson 1998- present

RECREATION

Tom Henderson, on the right, is pictured with Ken Kelly at Tom's superb ducket. He has raced pigeons for 54 years with distinction winning races in club, federation and being well placed in the giant Up North Combine which ranges from Berwick to North Yorkshire. Pigeons went hand in hand with leek growing but sadly of men like Tom Chester, Bob Farrington and Tom Dent only Tom Henderson flies the flag today. Lynemouth had a thriving pigeon club in the early years with Adam Scott, Frank O'Kane, Johnny and Andrew Gibbons and the Rainbow brothers all being prominent members. There are few pit villages of the population numbers akin to Lynemouth that can boast two Up North Combine winners – Tom Dent and Albert Wilkie. There is nothing more satisfying than breeding, conditioning and racing a pigeon to win at the highest level, rather like a racehorse trainer who wins a classic.

Lynemouth Institute

The Lynemouth Institute was built in 1925, but the General strike of 1926 delayed the opening until the Autumn of that year. Designed in Georgian style, Ashington Coal Company considered their project to be one of the finest buildings of its kind in the North of England.

Shown here is the institute shortly after completion in 1925 with the east bridge in the foreground. Mr Robinson Watson became Welfare Superintendent which included the Institute at that time, and he announced the furnishings alone would cost between £1,300 and £1,400. It was intended to play a major part in the recreation facilities of the new village. Unlike Institutes of the day which catered only for reading and billiards, Lynemouth's building was to be available to all of the people for many activities. By May 1927 only the main hall was furnished and open for dancing and roller-skating. It was then the cinema came to the Institute. This was well received by the villagers as previously they had to travel to Ashington by bus or 'tanky' (a steam engine which pulled old Victorian coaches). Controlled by Ashington Coal Company and financed by a Colliery Levy Scheme, the Institute was and still is the social centre of the village.

In 1934 the Institute parted company with the original Welfare scheme and incorporated a miners' levy solely for the finance of the Institute. Trustees from the coal authorities and unions have played a major part in the affairs of the Institute over the years, men like Jacky Sweet, Archy Herron and George Sweet.

From 1926 an operatic society existed and led by Mr Jack Balsdon until the war years. In 1945 a choral society was formed and principals were Minnie Dunn and Alf Cowton. The last performance was in 1973.

In 1938 a gymnasium was equipped and headed by Sgt Cairns of the Northumberland Fusiliers and later by Mr Neil, these activities ceased in 1972. Billiards and snooker are still popular, many fine teams have represented Lynemouth over the years. Bingo was first introduced in 1960 and still attracts many locals. Horticultural shows operated from the early years and an active leek club still exists. Many of the organisations have their headquarters here and private functions are a regular occurrence.

This is how Commander Kemp of Ashington Coal Company conducted his hive of busy bees, before the 2p children's matinee and handing out apples and sweets to all.

The Busy Bees

Fat boys, thin boys, everybody come,
Come and join the Busy Bees and make yourself at home,
And if there's not a seat for you, just sit upon the floor,
And we'll tell you little stories that you've never heard before.

We're just a hive of youngsters and we're called the Busy Bees,
And everybody's welcome just to join us as they please.
There's meetings twice a week, my lads, which starts at half-past-five,
And it's wonderful the many things that happen in the hive

It cost 6d admission for an adult to the pictures, although there were a few posh seats for a shilling. The first picture shown in May 1927 was *Rose of the World* a love and hate drama. The 'Gaiety' as the picture hall was known to the village people, was well supported and it was not uncommon for long queues to form and await its opening – at times it was necessary to book seats. The heydays of the movies were the 1930s, '40s and '50s, then Lynemouth's picture house suffered the same fate as many others who succumbed to TV and other leisure activities.

Lynemouth Gymnastic team played host to a German squad at Lynemouth Institute, *circa* 1951. Both teams were coached by Great Britain coach, Jack Flaherty. Included are: Bert McLeod, Harry Williamson, Peter Murphy and Jacky Brown. Colin Neil (Lynemouth coach) is front left. On the horse is Terry Dixon, assisted by Jack Flaherty.

The Institute snooker and darts teams competed in the Ashington and District League. Back: Bill Musgrove, Jim Fotheringham, Bill Brotherton. Front: Bill Tarbit, Jim Moscrop, Bruce Butters, Ralph Ritchie, *circa* 1940.

Senior snooker and billiards team receiving awards. Left to right: Norman Campbell, Bill Staines, Andy Brotherton, John Ogilvie, Joe Brooks.

Pictured in the big end of the tute on a night out are, left to right: Frances Hume, Amelia Hume and Jim Hume. A Social Club was formed in 1968 then in 1971 a new lounge opened by colliery manager, Mr Kay. The colliery levy scheme ended in 1993 with the closure of Ellington Pit by British Coal. This ended the Institute's colliery connection which lasted almost 70 years. Membership is now attained by private means.

These youngsters, *circa* 1985, from the Holroyd School of Dance at Lynemouth Institute gave up days of their school holidays to entertain Darby and Joan clubs in the Lynemouth and Ellington area. Many of the school's performances are for charity. The dancers are ably managed by Kathleen Holroyd and her sister Sadie Williamson.

Lynemouth And District Social Club

The Social Club committee first applied for a licence to trade in 1924. At that time it was a wooden hut sited at the east end of its holding, situated midway between Ellington Colliery and Lynemouth within easy reach of both villages. It was in 1926 when the club joined the Federation Brewery Chain and a long association would follow. The first steward was Mr Cuthbertson until 1928 when Mr George Brown took up the appointment. The old hut served its purpose, until a new brick club was constructed in 1933. It was Widdrington man Mr Telford who built this and was officially opened by Dr T. Skene.

This photograph clearly shows the old pantile roof club and the later additions to the east and north in the 1960s.

The Social Club always gave old folk an annual treat, this one in the Second World War.

An early committee – some of these men gave over 30 years service to the club. Back row: J. McPherson, R. Routledge, F. Johnson, J.G. Graham, T. Cochrane, E. Lowther, E. Sinclair, W. Crawford. Front row: T. Little, G. Little, C. Barras (treasurer), G.E. Summers (president), R. Lawson (secretary), T. Hodgson, J. Jenkins. Membership increased rapidly until 1960. At one stage in the 1950s over 700 members were recorded by secretary Jack Huntley. Situated between Ellington Colliery and the village meant that often men would call in for a quick drink on their way home from the pit, but this often led to more than just one and saw angry housewives invading the club in search of their men.

A new addition to the club in the 1960s was the lounge and the dance area. This coincided with the loss of key members when Lynemouth Institute gained a liquor licence in 1968. With the loss of older members, new trends in social entertainment and the geography of the club, resulted in a steady decline in membership. The death knell finally sounded in 1993 with the closure of Ellington Colliery under British Coal. As with many other coal field areas, clubs and institutes have ceased activities. This finally happened to Lynemouth in June 1996.

OF COURSE.

" It puzzles me to know how you, with your small salary, can spend every evening in the club bar, especially with a wife and seven children."
" Oh, Aa just leaves 'em aal at hyem."

Lynemouth Social Club Committee Officials, 1964. Back row: J. Laidler, J. Sandgren, S. Redshaw, J. Ross, T. Crawford, T. Scott, C. Sweet. Front row: J. Rirby, C. Taylor, W. Crawford (treasurer), R. Holmes (president), J. Huntley (secretary), J. Jenkins.

The club darts team shortly after the war years. Left to right: Bill Foster, Bill Nicholson, Herbert Fieldson, Isaac Nicholson, Jim Ross, Bob Nicholson, Jacky Gowland, George Reilly, R. Ogilvie, Alex Nicholson, Jim Laidler, unknown, Jack Huntley (club secretary).

Lynemouth Inn (Hotel), *circa* 1925. It was actually a hotel in the early years but used as an inn. A stable block was sited at the rear for weary travellers on horseback. It was designed in Tudor style and built by Ashington Coal Company in 1925. The first manager was Sylvester Strong. Being the only premises to serve alcohol within the village boundary, it was well supported and a home for many of the village organisations.

A critical moment in a game of dominoes, *circa* 1950. Landlord Albert Reed with cigarette, in competition with Don Lee. Albert Rhodes looks on with Eddie O'Keefe and Eddie Chrisp on the right.

The highlight of the early years was the visit in 1932 of favourite comedian Harold Lloyd who took lunch at the hotel. School children waiting to see their hero were unable to return to school at the appointed time. Their punishment from headmaster Mr Herron was an essay to be written on none other than Harold Lloyd!

The hotel hosted many functions, this a wedding tea, *circa* 1962. Pictured, left to right: Gus Sandgren, Dick and Will Simpson. In the 1960s and '70s the weekend dances at the hotel compared with many of the larger towns. The spit and sawdust image has never been lost. Once a home of the Catholic Church, it has in recent years seen extensive refurbishment. Its closure in a short while is owing to lack of support. Plans are now being considered by County Council to turn the hotel into a community centre with the aid of finance from Government sources. This would include a library, job centre, advice clinics, youth groups and computer skills centre run in conjunction with the school and Parish Council.

At the bar, *circa* 1955, are left to right: unknown, landlady Mrs Reed, Peter Dixon, Tony Johnson. Front: Albert Reed, Tom Lamb with the dog.

Leek Flower And Vegetable Shows

The leek was first believed to have been introduced to this country by the Romans during their occupation between AD 43 and AD 410. They would have been astounded had they known of the giant specimens produced today. Leek flower and vegetable shows first arrived in the north east pit villages during the middle part of the nineteenth century. After working underground men found relaxation tending flowers and vegetables, producing food for the table and later for the show bench.

The leek became a status symbol, each man attempting to grow the biggest and best leeks. Cultural methods changed, new strains evolved and growing systems a closely guarded secret.

Flower and vegetable shows were held in the village in the 1920s and 1930s, but it was not until the 1940s when the leek shows really came to the fore in Lynemouth.

Lynemouth Institute still retains an active leek club which includes lady members. Sadly Lynemouth and District Social Club closed its door for the last time in June 1996.

Jack Cochrane has won the Lynemouth Institute leek show three years in succession. Here is Jack on the left being presented with his trophies by Wilf Cowans and long serving committee man Tom Cowan. The Social Club was regarded as one of the most prestigious leek shows to win in the years leading up to 1970, as many as 150 stands of leeks were displayed in the September show. In 1952 Fred Brough, an Ellington Colliery coal face worker, created a world record for a stand of three leeks measuring 222.25 cubic inches. This was the fourth time in six years that Fred had taken first place at the Lynemouth and District Social Club. He had a problem as the oak writing desk he had won was almost identical to his previous year's award. Mr John Hudspith of Cambois judged the show and awarded runners-up to Fred's son Matty Brough, Tom Cooper, Will Hallowell, John Graham and Fred Mitcheson.

Fred Brough (left) and son Matty celebrate Fred's feat of breaking the world record while club committee man Henry Hanson looks on.

Eddie Liddle writes:

I was secretary of Lynemouth Inn (Hotel) leek club for many years. It was known as a leek, flower and vegetable show. We had an industrial section in the 1940s which included the school children and was organised by John Charlton.

We used the large upstairs room for our show which was held in September and was open all weekend. Monday was broth day when the women would use the unwanted leeks and vegetables to prepare broth for everyone at the hotel

We had a hard working committee then with men like Charlie Stephenson Davey Johnson, Bill Laidler, Bob McLean, Alec Aitchison, Bill Reed and Fred Chapman.

The leek show prizes were household goods which were an attraction for the women, who would enjoy seeing what their husbands had won for them. Prizes could always be exchanged with fellow members, or taken back to the Co-op and swapped for an item of equal value.

I finished as secretary in 1987 at the age of 76, with many happy memories to guide me, hopefully through my later years. After a time, the leek show lapsed then was revived again in 1995, but sadly the leek club disbanded.

Admiring the leeks, *circa* 1958, are: W. Stephenson, Bill Reed, Bill Jewitt, Fred Chapman. Right are: Davey Johnson, Eddie Liddle and Charlie Stephenson.

The show winner Ralph Gowland is seen here, in the Lynemouth Hotel, with his trophy while wife Mary holds the best leek in show.

Lying In State

They carried them from the trenches
And laid them in a row
Mutations of their former self
The work was hard and slow

For each a small white piece of card
Not names but numbers shown
Anonymous they had started life
In rank and file they'd grown

For two days they would lie in state
With hundreds filing by

Behind each one for all to see
Their honours displayed on high

Chemical burns and bruises
On some were clearly seen
While others skin was rough and torn
Where parasites had been

They scrutinised and placed them
Then drew aside to speak
A working man's club the temple
And lying in state, THE LEEK!

Matty Brough

Lynemouth And Ellington Colliery Band

Lynemouth and Ellington Colliery Band was formed in 1925. The first bandsmen mostly consisted of miners who had been members of colliery bands at some of the older pits which were at that time in decline. Moving to the new model village of Lynemouth, and working at nearby Ellington Colliery, gave hope for a bright future for these men and their families.

Many of the instruments were obtained on credit terms, the members giving concerts and various fund-raising activities to help pay for them. But then came the General Strike of 1926 and months of hardship for everyone, yet the band played on and in the years to follow went from strength to strength. Some of the original members were: Herron, Johnson, Lockyer, Green, Shears, Morton, Crawford, Simpson, Cooper, Waddle and Ward.

One of the original bands, *circa* 1929. During the 1930s and '40s there were new recruits to the band when men moved to Lynemouth from Durham, Haltwhistle and many other areas. This influx saw men taking up work at Lynemouth Colliery which at that time was starting to expand. Finance to support a band was given by miners. A colliery levy of 2d per week was deducted from their wages.

Right: The Picnic March Contest has been won and Jacky Liddell shows off the trophy to the crowds, *circa* 1950s.

The band pictured outside Lynemouth Hotel before leaving for a concert, *circa* 1950.

Joe Hogg remembers:

Bedlington Miners' Picnic was a special day in the bandsmen's calendar. Pitmen, friends and family congregating to celebrate the solidarity of the coal industry. The band marched from Ellington Colliery to Lynemouth where we boarded the bus to Bedlington Red Lion and from there to lodge headquarters at the Sun Inn. Women and children occupied the back room and many made their own private party. Then would come the march contest and the main parade of bands each one accompanied by trade union officials.

Banners flying proudly we made our way to the Picnic Field. Labour Party speakers would give their opinions on the coal industry and then we would be given the result of the band contest. We then returned to the Sun Inn where everyone met to take the bus home.

From Ellington Colliery, the band marched to Lynemouth Club where we stayed to relax and have a drink or two. From there we paraded to Lynemouth Hotel and by this time tired and weary, senses dulled with alcohol, there were some instruments played a little out of tune and marching slightly out of step. But no-one minded we were home, at the end of a perfect day.

The band has enjoyed success at the Northumberland Miners' Picnic event, winning five times, seven times second and ten times gaining third position. In the Coal Industry Welfare Contest we topped the third section, to move into the second section where we stayed for many years. In the *Daily Herald* contest held in London, Leeds and Manchester we qualified fourteen times. The City of Newcastle held a contest for ten years for bands from Northumberland, Durham, which we won twice.

The Northumberland Brass Band League was formed in 1948 and there were twenty-seven bands registered by the 1950s. Sadly there are now only five bands in this organisation. The demise of the coal industry is largely responsible for this, no longer is there financial support from local pits.

Thankfully Lynemouth and Ellington still retain their band and many fine players and conductors have progressed through their ranks. Conductors I remember from after the Second World War are: R. Routledge, R. Lowden, Joe Martin, Harry Galloway, Alf Cowton, Sammy Bond, M. Priestly and at present Keith MacDonald.

It brings back many memories for me when I see the band accompany the Lynemouth Children's Gala or marching before the Miners' Picnic, now held at Woodhorn Museum – it used to be me marking time and beating the big drum. The present band's headquarters are at Ellington Colliery, a more fitting place could not be found – the last remaining deep mine in the region.

Leading the band is NUM man George Sweet, Tom Chester (left) and George Whitfield (right). Supporting the banner in the front is Joe Nicholson.

Taking a break after a busy day are, left to right: Jim Baker, Florrie Graham, Joe Graham, Alf Cowton, Wilf Richardson.

RELIGION

Lynemouth Over 60s Choir was well represented and enjoyed success in competition, as seen by their awards, *circa* 1960. Back: Harry Williamson, Harry Yole, unknown, unknown, unknown, Mr Simpson. Middle: Mrs Huntley, Mr Scott, Mrs Noble, Mrs Laws, Mrs Wallace, Mrs Hogg, Mrs Kidd, Mrs Chrisp, Mrs Statham. Bottom: Mrs Ball, Mrs Freeman, Mrs Routledge, Mrs Paynter, Mrs Ward, Mrs Patterson.

The Beginning of a Church

In 1925 John Barrons, with then Primitive Methodist minister the Rev Barnes, went around the village and visited the members whose credentials had been forwarded to the Ashington circuit from their late churches and also the Ashington members who came to live in Lynemouth. There must have been about 20 members to begin with and they decided to form a church.

It was in the summer of that year that the first service was held in the open air. It was held on the green where the garage now stands, next to Smails the butcher. The preacher was Mr John Ritson of North Seaton.

From then on the meetings were held in the members' houses. Then the pavilion at the Welfare was acquired from Ashington Coal Company and services were held there until May 1926. The first Harvest Festival was held there and also the Sunday School was started on Sunday afternoons. There were also concerts held. One was by Cresswell Church Choir, soloists were Stan Cowton, Jack Scott and Ella Jacques. Chairman was Wm Scott from Ellington.

From May 1926 services were held in the school hall which was more like a chapel, very smart at that time more attuned to worship. The Sunday School still carried on at the Welfare.

The mind boggles at the thought of those members planning to have a church of their own in 1926, when the General Strike was at its height, but they did and saw the result at the stone laying by Lady Runciman on 31st March 1927. From then on the building grew apace and was opened by Lady Runciman on the 21st August 1927. Jack Chalders was the soloist. His solo was 'Open the Gates Of The Temple'. Mrs Sadie Brown played the organ. The teas for both occasions were held in the church hall kindly lent by the Church Of England.

The first Chapel members at the opening, 1927. Back row, second left, Mr Barker, second right is Mr Crackett. Middle row, seventh left, Suzannah Cooper, eighth Eva Cooper. Front row, first left, Mrs Barker, second left, Mrs Crackett, sixth Walter Fraser. Forefront, Raymond Barker, fifth is Willie Barrons artist and local historian who recorded the Chapel's history.

The members went to work with a will. It is an old saying the more debt the harder people work. It was many years before that debt was cleared. There were sales of work, concerts, plays and once a fish and chip supper was cooked in huge jam pans on the coal range in the kitchen. You name it, it was done at the Chapel to raise money. There was no caretaker, the women paired off and took their turns for the weekly cleaning, then got together about once a quarter for a good scrub out. Mr Barker did the stoking of the boiler. Once a year there was an old fashioned camp meeting held in the Dene, with a wagon for the speakers and the harmonium for the singing, and a great time was had by all. After the 1926 Strike there was an influx of miners from County Durham and Haltwhistle, as wages were higher in Northumberland than most coalfields, and so a few more members were added to the church. One of these was Mr Rice who was choir master for some time and Mr H. Yole who gave

great support to the Sunday School. He was also a local preacher. Miss Edith Foster was organist and head of the Primary Sunday School. Her father, William Foster, was trust secretary. He was also the first Sunday School superintendent. Other activities were the Girls' Life Brigade led by Miss Foster, and the Boys' Life Brigade led by Harrison Armstrong. The Chapel also had a badminton club.

The Chapel in 1930. Dr Skene's car is at the entrance to his surgery.

Hilda Knutton was the first nurse in Lynemouth and also a keen Chapel member, *circa* 1924.

Edith Foster's parents owned a shoe shop in Albion Terrace, while Edith taught at Ellington School and from 1926 at Lynemouth. The family became members of the Chapel in 1927. Edith held many official positions within the Chapel for as long as she was able until the 1970s.

The operetta Snow White performed by the GLB Girls at the Chapel, *circa* 1950.

Harry Armstrong (back) life boy leader, pictured *circa* 1950, at their summer camp at South Linton with, back row: George Mavin, Neil Taylor, Henry Cleverley, Colin Farrier, Ian Lunn, Fred Streener. Front: David Foster, Jim Clark, Roy Lunn, George Clark, Tom Horn, Derek Goodhall, John Streener.

Joan Cooper became one of the youngest GLB leaders. Jean is pictured at a leader's course at Seahouses, *circa* 1952.

The Co-op Town's Women's Guild met at the Chapel for many years prior to and after the war years, *circa* 1940.

Always a good following for the Sunday School from local children, ably managed by leaders at the rear, *circa* 1950. Left to right: Bob Farrier, Percy Armstrong and Jim Gotts

Lynemouth Day Centre

At Lynemouth Methodist Church there exists an activity that is a beacon of hope, at a time when many small churches in similar communities are facing closure because of dwindling membership, and lack of funds to maintain them. That hope is provided by the activity known as Lynemouth Day Centre which provides a secure environment on weekdays to elderly users. This facility has been in operation since 1984, initiated by the Reverend Bernard Nixon and his wife June. Co-ordinator in the early years was Nancy Wilkie, with support from the Borough Training Agency.

Tom Quenet the Methodist Minister has for ten years been involved with the Centre and is a source of encouragement for the young people of Lynemouth village, Tom is moving to pastures new. Gillian Thompson is now the Lynemouth lady co-ordinating the Day Centre, which goes from strength to strength, with local staff involved they know the people and their needs.

Tom Quenet pictured on his last day at Lynemouth Day Centre was presented with a miner's lamp in gratitude for his service to Chapel and Day Centre. Left to right: Pat Lawson (Church Council), Belle Reynolds (Church), Tom Quenet, Gillian Thompson (Day Centre), Debbie Campbell (Accounts).

St Aidan's Anglican Church

The building of the church was completed and a dedication service took place in 1925. Church functions were held as the chancel could be screened to allow this. In the years following, the interior was fitted out with panelling, pews and eventually an organ. Some of this work was carried out during the 1926 General Strike by the mining families with time on their hands. Rev Thomas Horsfall, Vicar of St Bartholomews Church Cresswell, donated the altar in 1926.

In 1932 a bell was presented to the church, this came from Cresswell Hall after the sale of the estate in 1924. The church was part of the Parish of Woodhorn until 1961 and its first incumbent ministers.

The first minister was Mr F.S. Moore, when an adjacent church hall was built in 1961 St Aidan's Church and grounds were consecrated and deemed a parish. The first parish vicar was Mr Alec C. Beniams.

In 1975 a special service was held to mark the 50 year celebration. The first baptism was held in May 1926, a baby girl named Marjorie Earsdon Lemin.

St Aidan's Anglican Church.

The play Shylock performed by the church members, *circa* 1945. Far left is Ken Paynter, fourth back is Rev Lappin and centre stage is Louis Stephenson.

Jack Simpson and Betsy Ward were the first couple to be married at Lynemouth Church in 1926 and spent most of their married life in the village. They received a Bible from the church with a commemoration to remember the first wedding.

Many pit villages had choirs, singing was a natural instinct born from the hazardous nature of the miner's occupation. Seen here is Lynemouth adult choir with Alf Cowton choirmaster in the centre, *circa 1964*. Alf was a bandsman and ran a choral society in the early years. Left front is Maisie Tait, second left is Willie Barrons and the men at the back are: Bill Stewart, George Getty, George Bell and Ernie Paynter.

The church choir was ably supported by the vicar Mr Dowling seen here far left, *circa* 1964. The other gentlemen are: George Bell, Malcolm Bell, George Getty, Denis Readhead, Alf Cowton, Archie Hyslop. The ladies are: Iris Musgrove, Nancy Routledge, Mary Furness and Mrs Graham.

Rest In Peace

When Ashington Coal Company built the village in 1923 a cemetery was included in their plans and maintained to a high standard. After Coal Industry Nationalisation in 1947 the deeds were retained by the coal company and a sum of money allotted to St Aidan's Church of England for the up-keep of the cemetery. This continued until the early 1960s, when a strain on church finances saw the Parish Council step in with grants of money for the private tender grass cutting. When funding ceased, moves were made in 1989-1990 for Castle Morpeth Borough Council to manage the grounds, however, without the deeds they said they could do nothing. The Church Ecclesiastical Council proceeded to obtain the deeds, solicitors costs being borne by St Aidan's Church, Lynemouth, Parish Council and St Aidan's Roman Catholic Church, Ashington, who held services at St Aidan's Church, Lynemouth. When the deeds were finally handed over the Borough Council were unable to take over the cemetery's management because of the cost involved in restoring a now derelict cemetery almost unused for burials.

In March 1992 Lynemouth Cemetery Care Committee was formed as a charitable trust, to manage the cemetery for the village, with pledged help and only £400 to hand. In April of that year a start was made with borrowed equipment. Help was sought from Rural Action and the British Trust for conservation in applying for grants from British Telecom Community Challenge. A sum of £800 was given by Rural Action for hedging and tree planting suitable for wildlife, and BT supplied £1,200 for equipment and fencing. The work was completed on 4th December 1994 with voluntary help of villagers, scouts, guides and Youth Club. The cemetery was again in use for burials.

Only a short popular walk from the village, relatives of the deceased are now able to tend to their loved ones graves. The saying around the village is people are now 'dying to get there' in the best possible taste say the Care Committee. A small income from burial and monument fees is providing the carers with a lifeline for the future, but without their vision and the volunteer assistance none of this would have been possible.

Volunteers all these men, including Matty Brough who took the photograph, who gave their time to the maintenance of the cemetery. Left to right: Reuben Davison, Jack Spratt, Phil Spratt, Jim Hindmarsh, Jim Graham.

Lynemouth Scouts

Mention scouts in Lynemouth and the name Tom Rankin is foremost. He was involved in scouting in Lynemouth in 1925 when meetings were held in the church. There is a record of reforming of the group in 1937. It was in 1952 when the present group was formed by Tom Rankin. The Anglican Church always maintained an interest with people such as Ken and Ernie Paynter, Bob Waddell, Bob Batey and Gordon and June Renwick who were active scout leaders. Brian Hume served as group scout master for many years before taking his present role as advisor and Council member.

The very first troop of scouts pictured here in 1926 outside the newly built church. The scouts were allowed the use of the cellar for their meetings. Centre middle is leader Tom Rankin and fourth middle the first Church Minister, F.S. Moore.

By the 1950s a new headquarters was needed and an ex-POW hut was dismantled and transported from Widdrington to the Lynemouth site at Boland Road. After its erection, an opening ceremony was held and included district officials. Seen at the opening are, back right: Andrew Hyslop, Gordon Renwick, Brian Hume and Bob Batey with the cubs and scouts.

The Catholic Community

The village Catholic Community have never had a church of their own in the village, Ashington St Aidan's being the parent body. In early years a house was used in Park Road for worship, Lynemouth Hotel was used in later years for services. With the advent of Christian unity the Anglican church facilities were available. An attempt was made in 1970 to purchase the West Green near Boland Road, with a view to building a church. This was thwarted owing to road access problems. Due to re-organisation of clergy, services are now held at Ashington St Aidan's.

Bishop Ambrose visited the church in February 1999 and met the local Catholic people. He is shown here centre middle with Father McKenna, third left. In front of the Bishop is Mrs Harrigan and to her left is Mrs Hindmarsh while Kevin Hindmarsh is second right.

Four Catholic ladies, on a trip to Lourdes with St Aidan's, Ashington, are pictured here taking a well earned rest. Left to right: Martha Waddell, Terry Foster, Betty Bell and Nancy McLean.

PEOPLE, PLACES
& EVENTS

Lynemouth had its own Auxiliary Fire Service during the war years. They had a depot at the Ellington Colliery, Dene House disposal point and practised at Ellington Bridge using water from the River Lyne. Incendiary bombs were dropped on Lynemouth during the war. Pictured at Lynemouth Farm are, back: Bill Reed Isaac Hall. Left to right: Bill Wilkinson, Mel Harvey, Tom Crosby, Andy Herron, Win Graham, Fred Chapman, Mary Rankin, Mr Common, Bill Routledge, Andy Elliot, Len Wilson, Sam Leader.

The Flying Doctor

Dr Thomas Skene arrived in Lynemouth in 1923, shortly after the first Ashington Coal Co houses had been built. He had studied medicine at Edinburgh from 1911 but left to join the Infantry as an officer in the Great War, serving in the Balkans and Mesopotamia.

Tom Kelly remembers that his grandfather allowed him the use of his living room at No 2 Boland Road as his first surgery in the village. In the early years, he was often seen on his rounds, on foot and later on an old bike which he propelled at a furious pace. And no wonder, as by 1924 there were 430 houses occupied in the village. At this time, and until the 1940s, it was not uncommon to deal with outbreaks of Diphtheria, Scarlet Fever, Smallpox and many other serious diseases.

He grew up with the village and its people and became involved in many of its organisations in the community. Dr Skene was a Scot, as were many of the other GPs in the Ashington Coal Company area, who were often called to attend serious underground accidents. He knew every child in the village. Tom possessed a great sense of humour, that endeared him to the mining people.

One incident I remember well was when my brother was ill and my mother suspected German measles. She closed the curtains as was the custom to exclude light from the eyes. Dr Skene burst through the back door, inquiring as to why the curtains were closed. My mother advised him that she thought my brother had German measles. Where on he opened the curtains saying, 'I'm the doctor, I'll make the diagnosis.' On examination, he quickly closed the curtains saying, 'You are quite right Barbara, the boy has German measles. You should have been a doctor, put the kettle on I could do wi a wee drop o tea.'

He became the founder of the Burns Society, Vice president of the Lynemouth & District Welfare Operatic Society, a JP and was also involved on the sporting side being on the Ashington Coal Company's Welfare Committee, representing Lynemouth. Being a fine speaker saw him in great demand for local functions where he was often the guest of honour. In the 1930s he conducted his surgery in what are now the present day reception rooms in Albion Terrace.

In his later years, in the 1930s, he acquired a large shiny black motor car, something he had always wanted. It stood outside and everyone admired its sleek lines and wood dash board. A far cry from those early years with an old boneshaker bike.

Tom Skene retired from practice in 1959 aged 74 years. His wife had died some years earlier and he left Lynemouth to retire in Norfolk. And so the curtain fell on a career that had spanned 36 years, all of those serving the people of Lynemouth, Linton, Ellington and Cresswell. Tom died aged 82 years at his son's home in Crosby near Liverpool in November 1967.

Jack Simpson remembers:

'I was born at No 7 Dalton Avenue in 1926, but by 1930 the family moved to No 38. Other than school, most of the time was spent in the Dene behind Eden Terrace leading down to the River Lyne. At that time the river was clear and clean with plenty of fish and swans nested on the banks. Near to the river mouth was a favourite bathing place – one piece costumes for men and boys then. One day, Ashington Coal Company fenced the Dene and brought in pit ponies for resting and recuperation, but they were too fierce to let little lads ride them. Occasionally men on horseback with a pack of dogs would hunt for otters by the river bank.

Lynemouth was a happy, clean crime-free village and nobody locked their doors – insurance and electric meter men had free access. Many tradesmen plied their wares. Jimmy Norman a fishmonger from Newbiggin had a wooden leg, he came on a horse and cart crying 'Calla Harin' and Mary Twizell sold fish from a huge basket strapped to her back. Smail the butcher had a horse and cart to trade and the Spanish onion man had a bicycle. The rag and bone man rang a bell – he gave goldfish for old clothes.

Twice a month coals would be dropped from a horse and cart outside each house and we earned a little pocket money shovelling them into the coalhouse trapdoor. The women were proud of their doorsteps and would yellow them with rock of ochre. Monday was washday when women would use a barrel of water for the clothes and beat them clean with a poss-stick. Few could afford shop bread so baking was done at home and often when visiting friends dough would be rising in front of the fire. In the winter many people made rugs or mats, my mother always had a 'proggy' mat out in the sitting room.

When Dr Skene got his first car, boys would line up early on Saturday mornings hoping to be picked to wash it. He paid generously 6d for the lucky ones. The school headmaster was the highly respected Mr Herron. Mr Reekie and Mr Wash were strict rather fierce teachers but at times human.

Mary Twizell a fisher lass from Newbiggin came to the village every week to sell her fresh fish. She kept a handcart in the hotel yard to pull round the streets with her goods and became friends with many of the villagers, who knew her as 'Wor Mary'.

The railway line that cut Lynemouth in two meant we didn't socialise with 'over the line kids' except to visit the Welfare. My uncle 'Sticker' Ward was the cricket team's wicket keeper and my cousin Jack, Will and Tom Foster all played football and cricket.

The men were always talking about their work at the pit, my dad and his marras were dedicated but I'm not so sure about the owners. I well remember one day coming out of school and seeing men three and four deep in a queue from the school to the church hall which had been set up as a temporary Dole Office. The pit was closed because bad weather had prevented the coal ships from leaving Blyth harbour. However, most of my memories are happy ones. It seemed like everyone helped each other in many different ways in what were difficult times. Perhaps my most pleasant memory is of carpets of flowers in the Dene – yellow when the primrose bloomed and blue when the Bluebells showed.'

Lynemouth policeman, Tom Foster, was awarded the Queen's Commendation for Bravery when he disarmed a man brandishing a double-barrelled shotgun at a house in Widdrington in January 1978. He was presented with his medal by the Duke of Northumbria in August 1979. Tom was a typical village 'Bobby' much respected by the Lynemouth people. His police home was always open to those who wished to share their troubles or to have a chat about village life. Tom is pictured with his wife, Joan, after the bravery award ceremony at Alnwick Castle.

This picture shows Lisle Downie operating a coal chute at the coal company depot at Dene house, prior to delivery to miners' homes by horse and cart, *circa* 1950. Lisle's other duties included that of surface horse keeper at Ellington Colliery.

From Pit to Police Chief

Bob Huntley's family moved to Lynemouth in 1934 from Ashington. His father was employed at Lynemouth Colliery as a check weigh man. Bob had by then left school and worked as a token boy at Ashington Colliery, from December 1934 to February 1937, he was then in the employment of Mr Cutter's office. He then transferred to the time office where he saw service until December 1938 when he joined the Metropolitan Police Force.

Bob Huntley on his appointment at New Scotland Yard.

Meanwhile he had completed a three year course at Ashington Coal Companies Continuation School. Bob was a keen footballer and played for Lynemouth, Ashington Surface and Ashington Electricians.

After initial training at Peelhouse he was posted to M Division Kennington until 1941. Wishing to assist the war effort, Bob joined the RAF Bomber Command. His duties included flying agents and spies to Europe and the Middle East. His duties as a Flying Officer was as instructor at Aylesbury. He had by then managed to find time to marry and on 19th August 1942 Bob wed Lynemouth girl, Dorothy Kelly, at Woodhorn.

A return to the Police Force in 1946 saw Bob rise quickly through the ranks – A detective at Peckham, Detective Inspector at Chelsea and in 1950 service with the Flying Squad, then Chief Inspector, National Crime Investigations and a return to Chelsea as Superintendent in 1966 and then the position of Deputy Chief Superintendent Number One Area West End of London in 1968.

Bob's progress continued apace when he was promoted to Commander West End and on to boss the Murder Squad in 1972. The highest honour came when he was offered the post of Commander of the Anti-Terrorist Squad.

In 1962 he was awarded the British Empire Medal for gallantry after disarming a gunman in a London Club and more was to follow when he was presented with the Queen's Police medal in 1971 for Distinguished Police Service. In his career Bob was commended by his Commissioner on 42 occasions and Highly Commended twice.

He retired from the force in 1975, having given 36 years service. A tremendous achievement for a young man who began his working life at Ashington Colliery. His experience was recognised by the BBC and they acquired his service as Chief of their Security reorganisation effort in 1975 where he was to see out his days until final retirement in 1979.

Bob Huntley had a book published in 1977, under the title *Bomb Squad* and a fascinating story it is. Bob and Dorothy are still active and live in the south of England returning to Lynemouth on occasional visits to relatives and the place from where it all began.

The Lynemouth I Remember by Bill Johnstone

Bill Johnstone emigrated to Canada in 1928 as did my father and many other young pitmen at that time, disillusioned with the conditions and lack of opportunity in the privately owned pits. Bill stayed and now lives in British Columbia. He recalls:

'This new village was to be a show-case to the rest of the country. All the roads, sidewalks and boulevards with trees were in place before a house was built. Then began construction. As the houses were completed the occupants moved in. My father was a deputy overman at Ellington Colliery and was one of the early residents of this brand new village. We moved from 105 Portia Street at the Hirst to No 7 Boland Road, Lynemouth in February 1925. My first impression of the house and village was one of amazement and satisfaction. We now had a much larger house, with hot and cold running water, a scullery where mother could do her laundry and a bathtub where the children could be bathed nightly without having to heat water to bath in front of the kitchen fireplace. The back of the houses had a paved enclosed backyard and it was here that the flush toilet and coal shed were built. The front of the rows were set back from the road to allow each house to have a fairly large garden each one being divided by alternate privet and laurel hedges. The company had made first rate sports facilities with an oval cricket pitch, tennis courts and soccer fields. There were places to stroll with the choice of the pastoral dene or the seaside trails to Cresswell and Strawberry Hill. Lynemouth was just a nice place to live and was in sharp contrast to the narrow crowded streets of the Hirst and Ashington.

Our joy, however, was to be short lived. We had only been in the house a couple of days and nights and the house was damp due to the newly plastered walls not being completely dry. To try to overcome this, mother lit a small fire in each of the bedroom grates. Then in the evening, when the younger ones of our family were in bed, my nine-year-old sister Jane got out of bed to place a blazer on the fireplace in doing so her night-gown caught fire and she was severely burned. She was rushed to Ashington hospital and despite the best care available she died the following day.

She was the first person to be buried at Lynemouth in the area designated for a cemetery. I believe at the time the ground had not been consecrated and the little plot where she was buried was given a special blessing and dispensation. This was a sad beginning for us in this lovely village. But mother being a devout woman was the anchor that kept us steady through this sorrowful time.

Although my tenure of Lynemouth was rather short, it was here that many of my memories linger. I was seventeen years old and going to the Colliery Continuation School in Ashington with Bill Grieves and Bob Snowball – lads whose parents also resided on Boland Road. Some of the people I remember who lived at Lynemouth in those early days were the Bob Tait family, Snowball, Common, Chapman, Sweet, Grieves, Rickaby, Hall and Kane all these lived on Boland Road.

One notable feature of Lynemouth was in the naming of the streets. In the Hirst, the names of the streets were taken from Shakespeare's plays – Ariel, Juliet, Portia, Katherine, Beatrice and Rosalind. In Lynemouth the streets were named alphabetically: Albion Terrace, Boland Road, Chester Square, Dalton Avenue and Eden Terrace. It was a different idea and one that left lots of room for the expansion that continued after I left.'

The Down Side

Much has been written concerning the benefits the Ashington Coal Company brought to its villages – the housing, recreation and education. People were moving into the model village yet some of the families were moving out, and not of their own free will. Charlie Foster started work as a putter at Ellington Colliery in 1911 and was among the first of its employees. After serving in the Great War with the Northumberland Fusiliers he returned to the pit in 1919, first as a hewer and then as a cutter man. He married and in 1924 moved into Chester Square. In 1927 Charlie fell ill with TB and spent many months in a sanatorium. After six months the Coal Company agent knocked at the Foster's door and Mrs Foster and her two children were evicted. That was the way it was in those days if a man was unable to work. The house was required for someone who could. This Dickensian practice continued until the Second World War.

Charlie Foster in 1929. His family still remember their chattels being loaded onto a horse and cart on eviction. Luckily a relative at Newbiggin took the family in.

The Dunn family moved into a newly built house in Henley Square in 1925. Father George was a stoneman at Ellington colliery. Like many others the family lived on very little and after the 1926 Strike even less. Worse was to follow when George died in 1932. Of the four children, George and Leslie were split from their family when evicted.

My Grandfather Will Taylor lived at 21 Eden Terrace. He moved there in 1924 from Radcliffe. My father Bill worked as a putter at Ellington Colliery but in 1928 left to seek a new life in Canada. In 1933 my Grandad was due to retire which meant he would be evicted from his colliery house as no-one else was employed by the coal company. My father returned home from Manitoba and back to the pit and kept the family home. In some cases Ashington Coal Company would insist that two men were required to work at the pit but at times they would waive this rule and school teachers and people with various trades have occupied coal company houses.

Bill Taylor on the right on his return from Canada in 1933, pictured in the west diamond district of Ellington Colliery. His two 'marras' are putters Jake Gallon and Joe Morris.

Sid Waddell remembers Lynemouth:

Sid Waddell alias 'The Lynemouth Lip' owing to his colourful TV darts commentary has many memories of the village:

'When I was about eleven, living at Cresswell Road, Ellington, we walked in fear of 'Lynemouth Lads' who, we were told, were ruffians and bullies. It was true. One day the Mitchell's held me down in a field and let a kid bounce a 'caser' football off my face. Luckily, my cousins Robert, Tot and Billy (hurricane batsman and fearless centre forward for Lynemouth) arrived, changed the rules and I hammered the kid.

In the summer of 1954 I became a Lynemouth lad myself. My dad had worked at Ellington Colliery since the age of fourteen and we got a colliery house in Dalton Avenue. My parents were both members of the Social Club and my mam loved to dance there on Saturday nights. Bob was a leek man – once coming 10th in the Club leek show. He was also a very good billiards and snooker player. My brother Derrick was an enthusiastic member of the Lynemouth School football team and once won first prize in the fancy dress on gala day (sports for all and sticky buns in a paper bag for the bairns).

I went to Morpeth Grammar School and played rugby, but also played football for Lynemouth Juniors. I trained for sprinting at the Welfare with the Hansons and other professionals. I also did weight training at the Miners' Institute with Colin Neil.

I would say the village was at its peak around 1963. There was full employment and I well remember playing bingo with my dad and his pals in the 'Big End' at the club on Sunday mornings. The place would be heaving and it would be full again for 'turns' and dancing at night. I also went to dances at the 'Hotel' – the Lynemouth Inn – and we attended Catholic Mass there as well!

My father worked at Ellington Colliery for 48 years, many as a salvage drawer. He was buried in a couple of times and his workmate was the famous Ashington painter Oliver Kilbourn. Bob did not want his son to go down the pit – so I was encouraged to study and in 1959 I went to Cambridge University.

My best memories of Lynemouth are of the New Year celebrations in the early '60s. After a good night at the club, we would go home till midnight. A few minutes before, a couple of us would go in the yard and when the pit buzzer blew we'd 'first foot' with a bottle of whisky and a lump of coal. Then we'd first foot all over to friends houses – drinking, singing and gorging on broth, pease pudding, ham, you name it. Once my pal Cliff Howe and I were still first footing on 7th January.

In a strange way the collective hardship of coal mining produced a rare humour and enjoyment of life in the village.'

Against All The Odds

At 6.10 am, on Thursday 18th October 1956, 26-year-old Archie Redshaw suffered horrific injuries in a roof fall at Lynemouth Colliery. It took workmates one hour to release him from a huge stone which measured 18' x 11' x 5'. At Ashington Hospital he was given blood and owing to his critical condition a top medical team received him at Newcastle Royal Victoria Infirmary. Archie had no feeling in his back or legs. His injuries included a broken spine, a bone splinter across the chord itself, broken coccyx, fractured ribs, and collarbone and a fracture to the base of his skull. There was also damage to his kidneys and bowels.

Archie was twice resuscitated during the eight hour operation, by all accounts he should not have survived, but he did. Two days later he was told he would be completely paralysed in both legs. His reply to the surgeon was this 'If Aa git haaf a chance Aal proov Yi rang.'

He was transferred two weeks later to Hexham Spinal Injuries Unit. During the journey he haemorrhaged and spent a further week in an oxygen tent. He pulled through once again, but his next fight was against withdrawal symptoms from morphine overdose. He experienced a little feeling in his right leg and was fitted with a calliper on his left and had plates inserted in his back. Through sheer determination, in June

Archie and his sister, Mavis, at the back door of No 2 Dalton Avenue shortly after starting work, circa 1946.

1957 he walked one vital step with crutches. Eleven months later he returned home to No 2 Dalton Avenue, Lynemouth. Owing to difficulties with the stairs, Archie, his mother and brother Les, moved to Widdrington, where he bought a derelict piece of land and had a bungalow built for his special needs. In 1985, fate had struck again and Archie was forced to return to Hexham General. A colostomy was required and he became so ill he was given little chance of survival. He returned home after six months, his spirit had won through again.

Archie has spent 10 years of his life in hospital since that black day in 1956. He shuffled the three paces to his back door and his eyes twinkled mischievously as he said to me, 'Aa telt that doctor Aa wud waalk yi see.'

'And so you did bonny lad, so you did,' I replied.

Archie on his feet again after his accident pictured at his new home at Widdrington, ably supported by Nellie Tunn on the right and her sister Betty Teasdale, circa 1980.

Sylvia's Story

My maiden name was Sylvia Mitchinson and we lived at 15 Kingsley Road, Lynemouth. My father, George Cummings Mitchinson, was a deputy at Lynemouth Colliery until 1966 when the mine went on fire and was closed down. After working on the 'shore' doing salvage he took retirement and emigrated to join me and my family in Australia.

My mother, Sadie Mitchinson, worked at the Lynemouth Institute as a cleaner for many years, not only cleaning the Institute but the cinema behind it as well.

I remember a small plump fellow who was the postman for many years, a friendly cheerful man who handed me my letters on the way to the bus stop. I think his name was Jasper and his catchphrase was 'Yi waant blaan up.'

I remember the coal being delivered to the back door by horse and coal cart and we had to shovel it into the coalhouse via a trapdoor in the wall.

There were several street parties celebrating the end of the Second World War. Bonfires were built in the back lane and in our case we burned a huge hole through the tarmac but no-one seemed to mind – we were so relieved the war was over. I think everyone went a little mad celebrating – dancing, singing and dressing-up was the order of the day. We moved to Lynemouth after the land mine was dropped but due to shortages there were still lots of houses with no glass in the windows.

I well remember the 'Big Snow' of 1947 when we were all snowed in for four days. The snow plough took three days to clear the road to Woodhorn – it was just as well we had coal to keep the homes warm. My mam baked bread for half the street – she was good at it and neighbours brought the ingredients for her to bake the bread for them.

Saturday night dances at Ellington Institute were very popular. A three piece band, drums accordion and piano pumped out the popular tunes of the day and Victor Sylvester tunes to dance to. I think all the local teenagers learned to dance there or at the Arcade at Ashington. It was quite a thrill to 'graduate' to the Arcade on a Saturday night, either rushing for the last bus at 10.50 pm or if

Everyone celebrated the end of the war with a street party in 1945. This one is at Albion Terrace and Dalton Avenue.

you missed that running along to the Colliery Station to catch the pit 'tankie' to bring us as far as Ellington and walk the rest of the way to Lynemouth. On summer nights we would walk from Ashington, buying fish and chips, or sausage patties and chips at the Arcade Fish Shop and eating them from the paper as we walked home.

The Lynemouth Dynamos Football Team was started to raise funds for the Lynemouth Men's Soccer Club. My mother was the goalie and I played either centre half or centre forward. We had Jackie Milburn and his colleague George Stobbart come more than once to referee our games. Jack once said on Radio Luxembourg that I was his most embarrassing moment. He was refereeing a match and two players collided and one was badly winded. He said: 'I know what to do when a man is winded but I was so embarrassed as I didn't know what to do with a female.' That female was me.

Many a professional runner trained at Lynemouth Welfare. My father had runners in training and I used to train with them. There were few facilities for females in those days. Many a good soccer player started in Lynemouth, Malcolm Musgrove being one of them.

One of my friends was Jean Hollamby, who lived in Park Road. She now lives in Ashington, married to a relative of mine named Robinson. I occasionally hear from her.

Ronnie Glynn also lived in Park Road – he became a jet pilot in the RAF. He married a local girl who lived further along Park Road and was a teacher. Ronnie Redpath and Don Heron went to Morpeth Grammar School as did Maurice Tweddle. Don Heron became a schoolteacher and Maurice Tweddle later changed his name to Maurice Hilliard and became an actor after attending the Sir Lawrence Oliver School Of Dramatic Art. He performed at Tynemouth Repertory Theatre before emigrating. Eva Ross, who lived near the Dene, became a nurse after studying at Guys Hospital London. Families named Birch, Tunn, Bickerton, Sweet, Ewart, MacLean, Blake, even though they moved away, spent their early years in Lynemouth.

Lynemouth Hotel was the venue for the Catholic Church. Services being held in the downstairs ballroom on a Sunday morning. It was a joke that on Saturday nights the local policeman would spend his evening in the bar and at 9.45 pm he would leave and put on his uniform and come back for 10 pm closing time. There were few cars in those days and he only had a bicycle but still commanded respect. I think his name was Willoughby.

The old mill road after the snow of 1947. Mrs Young is pictured taking a walk with son David when the road was cleared. Lynemouth Colliery can be seen in the background.

The Rescues

Right: John Henry Yole, 1886-1967. John married Ethel Collinson and moved to Lynemouth from Bishop Auckland in 1928 to live in Kingsley Road and worked at Ellington Colliery. A local preacher, he became leader, society steward and assistant secretary of Lynemouth Methodist Chapel

On the 13th April 1954 retired miner, 67-year-old John Henry Yole pottered in his garden in 2 Church Square. Suddenly Mrs Irene Tindale appeared running towards the river shouting to John to come as her daughter Cynthia had fallen into the river. He followed as quickly as his coal dusted lungs would allow him. Mrs Tindale had jumped into the tidal flow to save her child, but both mother and child became submerged. John entered the water and grasping reeds extended one hand to pull mother and child to the bank, and resuscitated the child who wasn't breathing. Thankfully the girl survived. Mild mannered John was honoured by the community at a village ceremony (right).

Bottom right: On the 21st February 1974 three Lynemouth pensioners received bravery awards for their heroic part in the rescue of retired miner Bob Gray from his blazing home at 6 Eden Terrace. Bill Taylor pulled Mr Gray from his fume filled home and along with Jim Floyd and Eddie O'Keefe beat out and ripped off his burning clothes. The three ex-miners were highly commended by police and fire brigade. The fire brigade used breathing apparatus to tackle the blaze and the downstairs was completely gutted. Sadly Bob died some days later in hospital.

Park View Sheltered Accommodation

Operated on a warden scheme run through Castle Morpeth Council, Park View provides a warm secure environment for the occupiers. Ably managed by warden Yvonne Casson and her assistants Jen Spratt and Heather Welsh, the complex has the benefit of a twenty-four hour alarm system, laundry, lounge areas, day room and kitchen with guest rooms and ample grounds and parking areas. Opened in 1987 it is built on an area which was once part of Lynemouth Welfare Park.

Shortly after the opening local MP Alan Beith called to meet the residents, *circa* 1987. Pictured are some of the first people to occupy the flats. Standing:

Mrs Hanson, Bob Jones, Peg Taylor, Joyce Getty, Alan Beith, Nellie O'Keefe, Yvonne Casson (Warden), Mary Ferguson, Martha Lowther. Sitting: Margaret Brown, Lena Green, Chrissie Moore, Muriel Thompson, Mary Gowland, Jean Stewart and Mrs Tait.

Left: Dr John Cash came to Lynemouth in 1962 and served the local people as GP until his retirement in 1994. Often he called to the flats to attend the older people. He is held in high regard by all the villagers. John is shown here with his wife Betty, on the left, being presented with gifts from Park View residents by Warden Yvonne Casson.

Right: There must have been something refreshing about Lynemouth, for all of its early doctors have served lengthy periods in the village. None more so than Doctor Brahma who came in 1967 and retired in 1996. He is pictured with his wife Liz at his retirement celebration at Park View and some of his gifts from the residents.

Many villagers had family photographs taken by keen photographer Jake Gallon. Here is an example of his work with the Taylor family of Dalton Avenue, *circa* 1945. Left to right: Nancy, baby Elizabeth, Marjorie, George and Keith. George Taylor

came to Lynemouth in 1930 and many of the family walked all the way from Durham to seek a new life in the expanding mining village.

Rob Brown at Lynemouth beach looking for a little fuel for the home fire

Right: Harry Hanson of Norwegian stock came to Lynemouth from America. He met and married Elizabeth Doleman and they were one of the first families to settle in the model pit village in 1923. They had a family of nine children five boys and four girls. The photograph shows Harry and Elizabeth with sons Ken, standing left, and Gus, right, *circa* 1938.

There was other means of travel other than the tankie to visit Ashington. This photograph of 1926 shows the service bus at Linton crossroads. That's little Mary Rankin at the rear looking out the window.

Tom and Ellen Simpson came to Ellington Colliery in 1912 when Tom started work at the pit. They moved to Boland Road, Lynemouth in 1932 when Tom retired from work aged 70 years. They are pictured here at the wedding of Hannah Simpson and Joe Readhead, *circa* 1931. Back, left to right: Tom Simpson (Junior), Will Simpson, Tom (Senior), Nellie, Ellen, Jim, Dick and Jack. The bridesmaid is Sadie Templey.

When the Duke of York, who was later to become King George VI, visited Lynemouth, he came expecting to see miners' hovels. He went on his way suitably impressed by the new model village. Lynemouth never did have the old 'Middens' or earth closets, but instead boasted outside flush toilets or 'Grand Netties' as some of the old folk remember.

SIGNING THE VISITORS BOOK

ARRIVING AT LYNEMOUTH INSTITUTE

H R H MEETS THE DIRECTORS AND OFFICIALS

INSPECTION OF ONE OF THE LYNEMOUTH HOUSES

District nurse Doris Forster or nurse Brotherton as she was known later came to Lynemouth in the 1930s and took over from Lynemouth's first nurse Hilda Knutton. She lodged with Mrs Booth until her marriage to local lad Andy Brotherton. Her area included Woodhorn Grange and extended to South Linton Farms. As midwife she brought many of Lynemouth's children into the world. Here she is with one of Lynemouth's babies.

The village had a well supported cycling club during the 1930s, '40s and '50s. Rain, hail or shine, it was out on the roads for a day's cycling. Shown here taking a well earned break are some of the members at Matfen, *circa* 1940. Second left, front is Bob Morton. Third right is Eddie Liddle.

Mr & Mrs Dick Spratt arrived in the village from Ashington in 1931 and they lived at 6 Guilford Square. There were five children: Florrie, Billy, Jack, Dick and Ken. Here is Dick in his pit clothes ready for a shift down Lynemouth Colliery.

Lynemouth, as other mining villages, was a tight-knit community. Every corner end was a meeting place to share the day's gossip. These ladies are shown outside 11 Ingleby Terrace, *circa* 1950. Left to right: Mrs Mavin, Mrs Taylor, Granny Pat, Granny Crosby, Mrs Fail. Front: Maureen Mavin, Laura Lathlane.

Lynemouth's ladies had many organisations – this group represents the ladies club seen on a night out, *circa* 1950s. Included are, back row: Mrs Bruce, Mrs Bergfeld, Mrs Bell, Mrs Proudlock, Mrs Straughn, Mrs Love. Middle: Mrs Willis, Mrs Neil, Mrs Lonsdale, Mrs Robinson, Mrs Chrisp, Mrs Gordon, Mary Scott, Mrs Bruce, Mrs Wharton, Peggy Holland. Front: Mrs Gowland, Mrs Thompson, Mrs Richardson, Mrs Davison, Mrs Taylor, Mrs Nicholson.

Three miners in work clothes (*circa* 1940s) may seem out of place sitting on sand dunes, but the explanation is simple. Blakemoor drift at Cresswell was sunk for man access only to reach Ellington Collieries outlying coal seams in the  early years. Ed Hanson (left), Buz Ogilvie and work mate take in a breath of pure air before descending into the darkness below.

After the Suez crisis of 1956 Prime Minister Anthony Eden visited many areas in the country. Lynemouth Colliery was chosen as the NCB's model pit to show the investment and confidence placed in the areas coalfield. Here is Anthony Eden (centre) accompanied by Donald Hindson and other coal board officials on a tour of the surface area.

The charges detonated and Lynemouth's water tower is falling, *circa* 1984. Built in 1920 the tower supplied the water for the village for many years. The water was pumped from Linton Colliery, filtered and chlorinated, and stored in the tower sited at the western approach to the village opposite Dene House. A part of the area's history has vanished.

This bridge was constructed in 1925 by the Ashington Coal Company to carry road traffic over their railway line. The bridge was demolished in 1992.

Lynemouth lady Margaret Cadwallender (Huntley) has served the village in the role of librarian for 25 years and the county library for 34 years. Margaret is hoping to retire shortly. The present library near Lynemouth School is expected to move to the proposed multi-purpose centre at Lynemouth Hotel. The photograph shows Margaret at the library reception.

The village's grand old lady, Mrs Jemima Sewell, aged 91, cuts the Coronation cake at the Chester Square party in the scouts hut, 1953. She was presented with flowers by Jennifer Gibbons and husband William, the oldest man, received a button hole from Miss Delyia Moore. Front, left to right: Jennifer Gibbons, Mrs Sewell, Delyia Moore, Mr Sewell.

A Whale Of A Story

There appears to have been confusion in various reports concerning the beaching of a sperm whale in 1822. The problem was the exact position on the beach where it was stranded. This was a vital factor if the whale was to be to be claimed by the landowner. My research shows that the mouth of the Lyne was where the event occurred and therefore on land owned by Mr R. Atkinson who possessed land in Lynemouth.

However, the actual killing of the beast, which measured 61 feet in length and 37 feet in circumference, was completed by a blacksmith in the employ of land owner Mr Baker Cresswell.

A dispute raged between the two factions as to ownership and then the Admiralty stepped in and claimed the prize for the Crown. It was indeed a prize as it produced nine tons of flesh and 158 gallons of oil, which would have been welcomed by either of the local land owners.

The jaw bone and other parts were later exhibited in the grounds of Cresswell Hall. The Hall itself was at that time in the early stages of building, and the bones proved an attraction to the visitors on the miniature railway which ran through the estate.

The probable explanation as to why they were displayed there, is that Lynemouth was only a small hamlet and had no place worthy to display the remains. Then we must consider the fact that the position of Ralph Atkinson, of Lynemouth, was that of JP and Baker Cresswell High Sheriff of the county. Whatever the reason there is little to see of the remains today, and what was an issue between the two parishes is no more.

Above: A drawing of the whale by John Foster.

Right: This photograph taken in 1927 shows the whale bones displayed on a plinth in the grounds of Cresswell Hall. Left to right are: Jesse Simpson, Tommy Simpson, Jack Simpson and Hannah Simpson.

Albert Wilkie in typical pose, 'Lynemouth's Lord of the Manor'. He guards the western approaches to the village. He converses on any subject from leeks to languages or pigeons to politics. The Wilkie family arrived in 1924 among the influx of residents and lived in Ingleby Terrace. Albert has the honour of winning Lynemouth Social Club's leek show three times during the halcyon years of the '50s and '60s and once owned a pigeon to race and win 1st Up North Combine – an area which stretches from Berwick to North Yorkshire and includes some of the best pigeon fanciers in the country. This was in 1973 and the race was from Beauvais in France a distance of 427 miles.

The Writer

There are many Lynemouth people who have progressed in their chosen field of work. One such man was Maurice Tweddle or Hilliard as he was later to become when he wrote under that name. He wrote several novels and the one probably best known to Lynemouth folk is *The Years That Were Summer*. In his work there are several times that people and places can be associated with his home village. Maurice had not forgotten his roots. After emigrating to Australia he returned to live in Morpeth but sadly died some years ago.

The Batsman

Tom Lister was noted for his stone wall defence when batting, when he went in to bat all his team mates went home, had their tea and went to the first house at the pictures knowing that Tom would still be at the wicket when they came back.

The Pay Check. Very few miners in the early years ever got the chance to progress in other fields outside of mining, simply because their meagre wage was needed to help the family survive and they would often work shifts of twelve hours or more underground. A visit to Woodhorn Colliery Museum will show the talents of the areas art and craftsmen, many now long gone. Walter Bell, a Lynemouth lad, and former miner left the pit to join the teaching profession. An accomplished artist he has drawn and painted many facets of pit life.

Miners need a sense of humour. The very nature of the dirty wet dangerous conditions dictates this, a kind of safety value to combat the claustrophobic effects of the pit. Jack Graham now 86 years old certainly has. He arrived with his parents and two brothers in 1929 from Haltwhistle to work at Lynemouth Colliery. He is seen here on the left with neighbour Arthur Cooper behind the privet treeman he has created and dressed by topiary methods.

The War Years

One clear cold January night in 1941 a German aircraft dropped a parachute mine on the village. The newly built Post Office in Albion Terrace was demolished and also Wilkinson's shop. Many houses in the village were damaged with some families being rehoused in nearby villages and towns. The school felt the effects of the blast and children took lessons at Lynemouth Institute which was later found to be structurally damaged.

Sadly, Mrs Athey was killed, her home was in Dalton Avenue near the explosion. Seventy-four people were injured mainly by flying glass. Dr Skene and his team of medics from the St John Ambulance and the Home Guards tended the wounded at a makeshift centre in Lynemouth Chapel for some time after. Many were referred to Ashington Hospital which was specially prepared for such an event.

Dalton Avenue shortly after the bomb dropped. The house on the left was Will Simpson's who lived next door to Mrs Athey, *circa* 1941.

Lynemouth and Ellington Home Guard at Ellington Colliery, *circa* 1940. Back, left to right: unknown, Tom Rankin, Bill Cleverley, J. Fotheringham. Front: Bob Sawkill, Lisle Downie, Jakie Gallon, Roley Chester. The company headquarters were at the Welfare Pavilion and met three times a week. Shooting practice took place at Strawberry Hill with hand grenade training at Duridge Bay. Often exercises were arranged with regular soldiers to keep part-timers on their toes, and weekend camps were organised. One night in 1942 Bill Musgrove was patrolling near the Welfare when a parachute mine exploded near the cemetery. He dived to the ground and thought one of his patrol had done likewise but landed on Bill's back. After a while he shouted for the man to let him up but there was no reply. Fearing the worst he heaved himself upright only to see a massive lump of clay fall to the ground. That had come from the explosion and was responsible for pinning him down.

Most of the villages had special constables during the war years to patrol the village boundaries. These are the Lynemouth and Ellington men who worked the area, *circa* 1940. Back: F. Pegg, PC Alec Bruce, F. Crawford, R. Tait, R. Lunn, W. Thompson, J. Simpson, R. Prior. Middle: J. Charlton, A. Reed, H. Crawford, T. Weddell, W. Simpson, R. Henderson, J. Henderson, Sgt Neilson. Front: J. Weir, the five others are from police headquarters.

Lest We Forget

The war memorial outside Lynemouth Institute is a dedication to the men and women of Lynemouth, Ellington and Cresswell who gave their lives during the Second World War. Miners were exempt from conscription as mining coal was a necessary occupation to fuel the war machine. However,

this did not stop villagers enlisting in the forces. And the canny lads and lasses that came home to a new beginning after the war years, most of the men to the pits at Ellington or Lynemouth, safe in the knowledge that they had given their best to the war effort. Many of the women had worked at arms and munitions factories, leaving their home village for months at a time. It is to all of these local people including those who served in the First World War that this section is dedicated.

Written by Iris Foster

I remember one summer night during the Second World War. I finished my day's shift at Ashington Hospital where I worked as a domestic. It was a clear, calm evening and still daylight as I started to cycle home to Lynemouth. When I reached Woodhorn Colliery I took the narrow path which leads to Woodhorn Bridge.

It was then I saw this solitary aircraft approaching very low from the direction of Newbiggin. I thought it had a strange sound and when it came nearer I knew it was a German aeroplane. Before I could act it swooped lower over the pit and there was a loud explosion. The blast blew me off my bicycle and I ended up on my back. I was shocked and dazed and lay for sometime. Then I saw the aircraft return over the pit and head out over across the sea.

It was said later the aeroplane was detached from its squadron and had managed to slip undetected through the Radar Net. However, it had been shot down by British fighters over the North Sea. I slowly made my way home very thankful that I was still alive. I met my boyfriend Bill Foster on the Windmill Road, he was later to become my husband. We had arranged to go to the pictures that night and he became concerned

Iris Foster (Musgrove) pictured with her bike during the war years.

when I hadn't turned up. He visited my home and found my mother worrying why I was late, and my dad was out on Home Guard Duty.

I was so pleased to see Bill that I cried tears of joy and relief. I will always remember that night, it brought the war a little closer to home.

Frank Wyness of Dalton Avenue joined the RAF at Cranwell in 1928 aged sixteen years. He took most of the prizes at Lynemouth school gala in 1926 and his fitness was to prove vital in the Second World War. He was first a navigator, then a pilot in RAF Bomber Command. He became the first person in Lynemouth to be decorated during the war, when he was awarded the DSM. A presentation was held at Lynemouth picture hall and the ceremony conducted by local dignitary Mr Ball. Frank became a member of the elite Caterpillar Club, a gold caterpillar with ruby eyes, which was awarded to aircrew who saved their lives by jumping from a stricken aircraft. He avoided capture to return home and fight again.

Frank Wyness.

Bob Wyness was born in Dyce near Aberdeen in 1880. As a young man of eighteen he joined the cavalry squadron of the British Army, the 9th Lancers, and saw action in the Boer War in South Africa at the turn of the century. He became an excellent horseman and eventually gained the rank of Squadron Sergeant Major. Bob fought in the First World War with the 7th reserve regiment, where he was engaged in some of the major battles. His expertise with horses was recognised when requested to train King Edward VII's steed in Ireland. In gratitude for his service he was given a personal snuff box. Bob was given the

Bob Wyness (4th left facing) in South Africa, 1908.

honour of riding alongside the King's carriage at his funeral ceremony.

In 1921 he was asked to instruct the Northumberland Hussars in the art of horsemanship and this is why he appeared in this region. His distinguished career in the cavalry came to an end when he left in 1923 to take up an appointment with Ashington Coal Company at its new village in Lynemouth. Every evening Bob would appear at dusk on his bike carrying a long pole with a hook on the end. This was used to operate a switch on the lamppost at every street corner and provide light for the village. That he never missed any of the switches was due to his cavalry training where he was a champion at the art of tent pegging, a sport designed to test the skills of horsemen – Ashington Coal Company had chosen a professional for the job. His other duties included that of sexton, gardener and custodian of the private dene.

Margaret Nicholson

Margaret Nicholson lived with her parents, sister and three brothers at 27 Dalton Avenue in the village. She worked in Lynemouth Co-op grocery department before joining the WRENS in 1943. After training in accounts she volunteered for overseas duty and was posted to the Middle East based in Port Said which was her station for the duration of the war. In 1945, Heading WREN Margaret was requested to assist in Malta, including visits to Sicily and Beruit in her travels. It was 1947 when she was discharged and returned home to Lynemouth before working for Ashington Co-op.

Left: Margaret after enlisting in 1940.

John Edward Gladstone Foster, 1898-1980

Johnny was the youngest of the five Foster brothers. He joined the army to fight in the Great War. Of the five who all worked at Ellington Colliery (Tom, George, Charlie, Chris and Johnny), Chris was killed in action in 1916. He was to fall on his twenty-first birthday, one of many brave lads who gave their lives for the cause. Johnny returned to work at Ellington Colliery after his Battalion of the Durham Light Infantry dispersed on 8th February 1919. He married Nellie Simpson and they lived in Dalton Avenue for many years.

Fred Harding lived with his parents, sister and brother at 3 Guilford Square. He started work at Lynemouth Colliery in 1934 aged fourteen years. A member of the territorial army, Fred joined the 7th Battalion Northumberland Fusiliers in 1939. A machine gun crew member, he saw bitter fighting after Dunkirk on the east coast of France. Short of ammunition, many of his friends were killed and Fred was taken prisoner. He was marched for three weeks with thousands of French and English soldiers, often without food or water, to the salt mine prison of Mentroda in Germany. Fred came home in 1945 and married local lass Emily Prior at Cresswell Church on 22nd September 1945.

Fred and Emily Prior on their wedding day. The bridesmaids are, left to right: Elsie Prior, Freda Chapman, Brenda Houlison, Margaret Charlton. Best Man was Cecil Wood.

Archie Herron, one of a family of seven children, lived in Boland Road and worked at Ellington Colliery when he enlisted at seventeen years of age in the Royal Marines in 1936. He joined the gunnery crew of HMS Ro*yal Sovereign* in 1938 and in 1939 and 1940 the ship was active escorting North Atlantic convoys. The *Royal Sovereign* then transferred to the Eastern Mediterránean when Italy entered the war. In 1941 Archie served with HMS *Anson* providing safe passage for Arctic convoys. By this time he was promoted to Corporal. In

1945 he became a Physical Training Instructor and by the end of his term of duty in 1948 gained the rank of Colour Sergeant. Returning home to Lynemouth saw Archie return to the pit at Ellington Colliery until retirement.

Right: HM King George VI inspecting Royal Marines HMS *Anson*. Archie is second right.

Charles Dawson

Charlie was 23 years old when he enlisted with the Royal Navy in July 1939. In 1941, as a stoker aboard HMS *Manchester,* his ship was torpedoed when escorting a Malta convoy, but managed to reach Gibraltar. On the 13th August 1942 the *Manchester* was again struck by a U-boat torpedo and sank. Charlie spent eleven hours in the Mediterranean oiled and weary before being picked up and taken to Gibraltar.

He took the plunge again in 1943, but this was for a lifetime when he married Linton lass Ruth Dawson when his new ship HMS *Brecon* was being refitted in Newcastle. Further action aboard *Brecon* came at the Sicily landings, Anzio and, in 1944, Malta. Charlie, now a petty officer, left the service in 1948 and as most of the lads, back to the pits and Lynemouth.

Right: Charlie pictured in Philadelphia in 1942 during his ships refit after being torpedoed.

Right: Harry Bryan escorting an overland convoy, *circa* 1944. Harry, a genial Irishman, joined the East Lancashire regiment in 1939. He arrived in Lynemouth when stationed nearby and met and married local lass Mary Rankin. Joining the elite commandos saw Harry in action world-wide until his return to the village after the war. He worked at Ellington Colliery as a deputy until retirement. He became a key figure in organising the children's gala. He has more than earned the right to become an adopted Geordie.

We Shall Remember Them

I was ever a fighter
The best and the last
I would hate that death
bandaged my eyes and forbore
Then bade me creep past.

Left to right: John Sandgren, Tommy O'Keefe, Fred Harding and Herby Fieldson remember fallen comrades on Armistice Day at the Lynemouth Memorial.

The first co-ordinator, staff and users of the original Lynemouth Day Centre.

As we enter the twenty first century what of the future prospects for Lynemouth? Gone are the heady years when coal was king and employment levels were high. There is now 30% unemployment in the village and the population is at its lowest since 1941. Where will the young folks find jobs? Will there be employers willing to put down roots just as Ashington Coal Company did at the turn of the century? Only time will tell. The wheel has turned full circle since 1923 when miners and their families came from near and far to seek a new beginning in the model village and find work at the two pits of Ellington and Lynemouth. I think it fitting to end with a quote made by Dr Skene shortly after his last baby clinic in 1959. 'They are fine people here I have lived and worked amongst them for 36 years and regard them as my friends. I will be sorry when the day comes for me to leave.'

The People's History

To find out more about this unique series of local history books – and to receive a catalogue of the latest titles – send a large stamped addressed envelope to:

The People's History Ltd. Suite 1, Byron House
Seaham Grange Business Park, Seaham
County Durham, SR7 0PY

or visit us on our website at:

www.thepeopleshistory.com